I0411666

United States
Department of
Agriculture

Forest Service

Forest
Products
Laboratory

Research
Paper
FPL–RP–625

Improved Utilization of Small-Diameter Ponderosa Pine in Glued-Laminated Timber

Roland Hernandez
David W. Green
David E. Kretschmann
Steven P. Verrill

Abstract

This study involved the evaluation of ponderosa pine glulam made from lumber that was sawn from a small-diameter timber resource. Two different glulam beam depths were evaluated: 8 and 13 laminations. A comprehensive glulam test program was conducted to evaluate edgewise and flatwise bending, shear, and tensile strength. Beam deflection was measured and a variety of glulam MOE values were determined. The calculated design values for various mechanical properties of this new ponderosa pine glulam beam combination were compared to the published design values of the L3 glulam combination. Using mechanically graded lumber in the glulam combination resulted in a structural member that efficiently utilized this small-diameter ponderosa pine resource. The calculated design values of this new glulam combination are a significant improvement over the published design values of the all ponderosa pine L3-grade combination that is currently available in the standards.

Keywords: ponderosa pine, glued-laminated, glulam, small-diameter, timber, juvenile wood

April 2005

Hernandez, Roland; Green, David W.; Kretschmann, David E.; Verrill, Steven P. 2005. Improved utilization of small-diameter ponderosa pine in glulam timber. Res. Pap. FPL-RP-625. Madison, WI: U.S. Department of Agriculture, Forest Service, Forest Products Laboratory. 38 p.

A limited number of free copies of this publication are available to the public from the Forest Products Laboratory, One Gifford Pinchot Drive, Madison, WI 53726–2398. This publication is also available online at www.fpl.fs.fed.us. Laboratory publications are sent to hundreds of libraries in the United States and elsewhere.

The Forest Products Laboratory is maintained in cooperation with the University of Wisconsin.

Contents

Executive Summary

The study reported here involves glued-laminated (glulam) timber members made entirely from ponderosa pine lumber harvested from a small-diameter timber resource. The primary objective was to develop an efficient glulam combination utilizing ponderosa pine for all laminations. Allowable properties were calculated from test results for modulus of elasticity (MOE), edgewise allowable bending strength (F_{bx}), flatwise allowable bending strength (F_{by}), allowable tensile strength parallel to the grain (F_t), and allowable shear strength (F_{vx}).

Preliminary analysis of existing ponderosa pine data showed that two E-rated grades could be targeted for the outer laminations and a visual No. 2 grade for the core laminations. The E-rated grades had an average MOE of 1.4×10^6 lb/in^2 (1.4E). The edge-knot (EK) grades were 1/4- and 1/2-edge knot. The glulam combination was designed with 15% 1.4E–1/4EK lumber in the bottom tension laminations and 15% 1.4E–1/2EK lumber in the top compression laminations. The remaining 70% was No. 2 grade core laminations. This targeted glulam combination could be made entirely from No. 2 and better grade lumber, an efficient utilization of the ponderosa pine resource.

Ponderosa pine lumber was cut from small-diameter trees harvested from the Apache–Sitgreaves National Forest in eastern Arizona. The lumber was initially graded as Standard and Better, kiln dried, and surfaced on four sides. Initially, the 7,972 pieces of lumber were processed through a continuous lumber tester and sorted into four grade classes. The lumber was also visually graded to determine if it met laminating stock criteria (wane, warp, and/or skip) and then sorted into either 1/4- or 1/2-edge-knot classification.

Glulam members were manufactured with 8 or 13 laminations for subsequent laboratory testing at the Forest Products Laboratory. Strength and stiffness were measured for each test orientation, and allowable properties were calculated.

The experimentally determined allowable properties of the glulam combination were generally higher than those of the all-L3 homogeneous combination currently available in the glulam standards. We conclude that mechanical lumber grading techniques can be used to obtain an efficient glulam combination with marketable design properties.

A comparison of the results obtained for 8- and 13-lamination glulam members confirmed that the industry standard volume effect exponent of 0.10 is valid for this data.

SI conversion table

Inch–pound unit	Conversion factor	SI unit
inch (in.)	25.4	millimeter (mm)
foot (ft)	0.3048	meter (m)
pound force/square inch (lb/in^2)	6.894	kilopascal (kPa)
pound force/square foot (lb/ft^2)	47.88	pascal (Pa)

Improved Utilization of Small-Diameter Ponderosa Pine in Glulam Timber

Roland Hernandez, Research Engineer
David W. Green, Supervisory Research Engineer
David E. Kretschmann, Research Engineer
Steven P. Verrill, Research Statistician
Forest Products Laboratory, Madison, Wisconsin

Background

The USDA Forest Products Laboratory currently has a research initiative to aid in the management of dense-growth forests in the western and southwestern United States. Approximately 39 million acres of ponderosa pine forests need thinning of small-diameter trees to reduce the fuel load created by this dense undergrowth (Forest Products Laboratory 2000). One research objective is to find economical and technically feasible value-added uses for the removed material. Value-added applications will help offset forest management costs, provide economic opportunities for rural forest-dependent communities, improve forest health, and reduce the severity of future forest wildfires. Recent research on structural applications has involved the development of kiln drying procedures to reduce warping and the evaluation of grades and characteristics of structural lumber sawn from small-diameter wood. The project reported here was initiated to evaluate the technical feasibility of utilizing ponderosa pine (*Pinus ponderosa*) in structural glued-laminated lumber (glulam).

To best utilize small-diameter ponderosa pine in glulam, information is needed on the mechanical properties of solid-sawn lumber processed from this resource. This information will be vital in developing a new glulam combination that could potentially be included in existing glulam standards.

Properties of Ponderosa Pine Lumber

The properties and yield of lumber cut from small-diameter ponderosa pine trees are a function of the diameter and age of the trees and the conditions under which the trees are grown. The primary grade-determining factor for this lumber, other than knots, is drying degrade, which is caused by warp (Simpson and Green 2001). A major cause of warp in ponderosa pine lumber is juvenile wood, which can constitute approximately the first 20 to 25 years of tree growth (Voorhies and Gorman 1982). Ponderosa pine is only moderately tolerant of shade; it grows rapidly until the upper canopy closes. Because of this growth characteristic, a considerable portion of a ponderosa pine log consists of juvenile

wood. The presence of juvenile wood creates a challenge for utilization.

Juvenile wood can be thought of as the "core" wood, the material closest to the pith (Fig. 1). Trees produce juvenile wood in the early growth period. The characteristics of the wood change markedly in each successive annual growth ring. During a transition period from approximately 5 to 20 years of age, wood characteristics gradually improve until they become relatively constant. This latter material is known as mature wood. In conifers, juvenile wood has lower strength, lower specific gravity, thinner cell walls, lower cellulose content, and a lower percentage of latewood compared with that of mature wood. Juvenile wood also has higher longitudinal shrinkage, more compression wood, a greater fibril angle, and higher lignin content.

Because ponderosa pine is shade intolerant (Burns and Hinkala 1990), one would not expect to find much difference in the volume of juvenile wood in trees growing in suppressed stands than in trees grown in plantations (other growth factors being equal). Recent studies support this assumption.

Small-diameter ponderosa pine from an approximately 35-year-old stand near Emmett, Idaho, yielded virtually no lumber that would grade as Select Structural (Table 1); about 13% of the wood was graded as No. 2 and better (Gorman and Green 2000). The logs for this study were obtained by thinning from below, which removed the poorer quality trees. Material thinned from a 45-year-old second-growth stand near Grangeville, Idaho, gave a 47% yield of No. 2 and better lumber, but less than 1% Select Structural (Erickson and others 2000). Even lumber sawn from suppressed trees (diameter ≤ 16 in.) from a 90- to 100-year-old stand in Flagstaff, Arizona, produced less than 3% yield of Select Structural grade lumber (Lowell and Green 2000).

The Emmett study also yielded information on mechanical properties (Gorman and Green 2000), which allowed us to compare the performance of lumber from that small-diameter resource to ponderosa pine lumber evaluated in the 1987 In-Grade Testing Program (Green and Evans 1987).

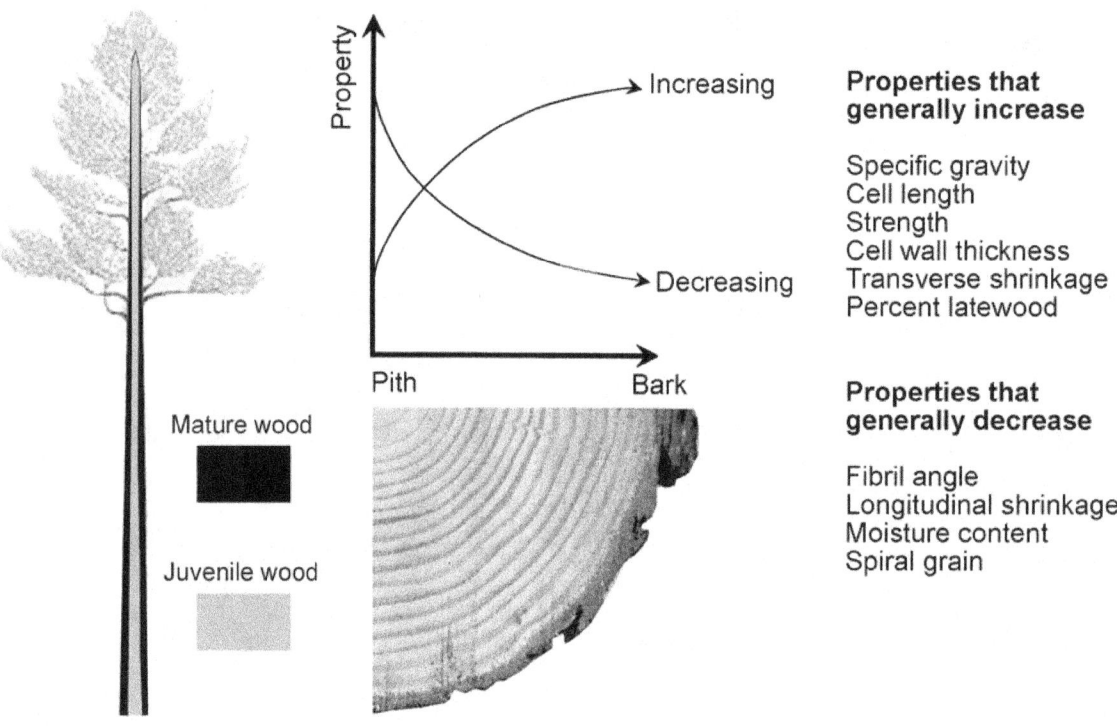

Properties that generally increase

Specific gravity
Cell length
Strength
Cell wall thickness
Transverse shrinkage
Percent latewood

Properties that generally decrease

Fibril angle
Longitudinal shrinkage
Moisture content
Spiral grain

Figure 1—Effect of juvenile wood on physical and mechanical properties.

Table 1—Grade yield of ponderosa pine from small-diameter trees

Grade[a]	Yield (%)		
	Emmett, ID (plantation)	Grangeville, ID (plantation)	Flagstaff, AZ (suppressed)
SS	0	0.2	2.4
No. 1	1.6	14.0	4.9
No. 2	11.4	33.2	26.7
No. 3	31.9	3.2	32.3
Economy	55.1	49.4	33.7

[a] SS is Select Structural.

The lumber tested in the In-Grade Testing Program was gathered from larger-diameter resources and likely did not contain as large a percentage of juvenile wood. Table 2 summarizes modulus of elasticity (MOE) data for both the Emmett study and the In-Grade Testing Program. Although only the No. 2 grade 2 by 4 lumber could be compared directly, the data suggest that MOE properties are slightly lower (approximately 10% at the mean) for ponderosa pine lumber processed from small-diameter trees. (Note: 2 by 4 refers to lumber with nominal dimensions of 2 by 4 in.)

In Table 3, a similar comparison was made for modulus of rupture (MOR) of No. 2 grade ponderosa pine lumber. Once again, only the No. 2 grade lumber could be compared

directly; the difference in strength was much more dramatic than the slight difference found for MOE. The MOR of the lumber from the In-Grade Testing Program was approximately 36% higher (mean) than the lumber from the Emmett study. This significant difference was likely due to the visually observed higher occurrence of juvenile wood in the Emmett lumber.

Thus, based on these past studies, lumber processed from small-diameter thinnings could be expected to possess significantly lower strength properties and slightly lower stiffness properties than lumber processed from larger-diameter trees harvested under normal logging conditions. Mechanical grading will add value to the graded lumber and improve yields, because visual grading of this resource can result in non-conservative design values. These facts strongly suggest that mechanical grading techniques should be considered when developing structural wood products from small-diameter ponderosa pine lumber.

Ponderosa Pine in Existing Glulam Standards

In existing glulam standards (AITC 2004), the two most common species groups of lumber used as laminating stock are Douglas Fir and Southern Pine. Ponderosa pine lumber is referenced in this glulam standard as part of a species group called Softwood Species. Laminating lumber belonging to

Table 2—Modulus of elasticity properties of ponderosa pine 2 by 4 lumber[a]

Grade	MC (%)	SG	Emmett, ID data				In-Grade data	
			MOE_{edge} (10^6 lb/in²)		MOE_{tv} (10^6 lb/in²)		MOE_{edge} (10^6 lb/in²)	
			Mean	SD	Mean	SD	Mean	SD
SS	—	—	—	—	—	—	1.129	0.19
No. 1	11.1	0.36	0.959	0.20	0.927	0.20	—	—
No. 2	10.9	0.35	0.877	0.19	0.855	0.18	0.976	0.18
No. 3	11.4	0.35	0.854	0.22	0.820	0.21	—	—

[a]MC is moisture content, SG is specific gravity (ovendry weight and volume at test MC), SD standard deviation.

Table 3—Modulus of rupture properties of ponderosa pine 2 by 4 lumber

	MOR (lb/in²)					
	Emmett, ID data			In-Grade data		
Grade	Mean	SD	5th percentile	Mean	SD	5th percentile
SS	—	—	—	7,510	1,700	4,320
No. 1	4,450	1,370	2,700	—	—	—
No. 2	3,880	1,410	2,050	5,290	2,100	2,650
No. 3	3,430	1,260	—	—	—	—

the Softwood Species group has relatively lower physical and mechanical properties than Douglas Fir and Southern Pine. For this reason, Softwood Species are only allowed in homogeneous glulam combinations made from E-rated laminations ranging from an average MOE of 1.6 to 2.1 $\times 10^6$ lb/in², as well as in homogeneous L3 visual combinations. Prior to the 2004 version of the AITC 117 glulam standard, Softwood Species were allowed in the core laminations of glulam beams made with Douglas Fir in the outer laminations. However, these types of glulam combinations were considered over-stressed in the outer laminations because of the low-grade core laminations, and thus they were removed from the standard.

Because of the relatively low mechanical properties of ponderosa pine, this species is practically disqualified as a viable source of E-rated laminating stock in the 1.6E to 2.1E range. As Table 2 indicates, ponderosa pine cannot achieve these MOE levels. In addition, the National Design Specifications (NDS 1997) publishes a design MOE value of only 1.2 $\times 10^6$ lb/in² for the Select Structural grade for Softwood Species.

This means that the only current glulam combination that can be made with 100% ponderosa pine is the homogeneous L3 visual grade combination.

The design values for the homogeneous L3 grade ponderosa pine glulam combination (Softwood Species) are as follows:

Modulus of elasticity, MOE	1.0 $\times 10^6$ lb/in²
Edgewise allowable bending strength (horizontally laminated), F_{bx}	725 lb/in²
Flatwise allowable bending strength (vertically laminated), F_{by}	800 lb/in²
Allowable tensile strength, F_t	525 lb/in²
Allowable shear strength, F_{vx}	195 lb/in²

Objectives and Scope

The objectives of this study were to develop an efficient glulam combination, with all laminations utilizing ponderosa pine lumber, and to evaluate test beams experimentally for MOE, F_{bx}, F_{by}, F_t, and F_{vx}. A single glulam combination was targeted: 15% high-stiffness laminations were used for the top and bottom layers; the remaining core laminations were equivalent to a No. 2 visual grade. Two beam depths were targeted for testing: 8 and 13 laminations. The 8-lamination beam was targeted for the F_{bx} and F_t tests and the 13-lamination beam for the F_{bx}, F_{by}, and F_{vx} tests. A total of 15 beams were targeted for each mechanical property group, for a total of 75 strength tests. MOE was calculated in each test, based on measured loads and deflections. The mechanical property test data provided in this report will serve as the basis for inclusion of a new all ponderosa pine glulam combination into existing glulam standards.

Experimental Design

Targeted Ponderosa Pine–Glulam Combination

Because past research shows low yields of Select Structural grade ponderosa pine lumber, we targeted the utilization of laminating grades that do not require stringent edge-knot criteria. This would permit ponderosa pine to be harvested from most areas of the country, including small-diameter resources.

Typically, outer laminations of E-rated glulam combinations are designed with 1/6 edge-knot (1/6EK) restrictions (AITC 2004). However, because of the low yields that would be expected with this grade of lumber, we designed the test beams to require only a 1/4 edge-knot (1/4EK) restriction in the outer tension zone and a 1/2 edge-knot (1/2EK) restriction in the outer lamination grades in the compression zone. For the core laminations, a No. 2 visual grade was targeted. This design allowed for the entire glulam combination to be manufactured with No. 2 and better grade lumber.

For laminating lumber, we evaluated the possibilities of targeting MOE levels of as high as 1.6×10^6 lb/in^2 for the outer laminations. However, based on the results shown in Table 2, we determined that a 1.4E lumber grade would be the highest MOE level that could be achieved with reasonable yields.

Based on these resource limitations, the resulting glulam combination would have E-rated grades of 1.4E–1/4EK in the outer tension zone, 1.4E–1/2EK in the outer compression zone, and No. 2 visual grade lumber in the core laminations. Furthermore, the 1.4E lumber grades occupied only the top and bottom 15% of the laminations in the general glulam combination.

With the general glulam combination established, an analysis was conducted using the industry standard ASTM D 3737 (ASTM 2000a). This involved estimating the properties of the targeted lumber grades (Table 4). These estimated properties were based on field data that had been gathered by quality control inspectors of the American Institute of Timber Construction (AITC), as well as past information for other species of E-rated lumber having similar edge-knot criteria. The properties included MOE, knot size characteristics, minimum bending strength ratios, and bending stress indices.

Development of Glulam Combination

Based on the lumber properties in Table 4, an analysis was conducted using ASTM D 3737 (ASTM 2000a) procedures to determine a technically feasible glulam combination made from all ponderosa pine laminations. Two beam depths were targeted, both to be manufactured with 2 by 4 lumber. The two combinations shown in Figure 2 were developed on the basis of this analysis.

The bottom tension zone consisted of 15% 1.4E–1/4EK grade, the top compression zone of 15% 1.4–1/2EK grade, and the remaining portion of No. 2 grade lumber. The 12-in.-deep 8-lamination beam shown in Figure 2a represents a potentially common size of beam that could be used in structural applications such as headers for garage doors and large windows. The 13-lamination beam represents the critical combination for the 15% outer zones. A 13-lamination beam requires 1.95 laminations of depth for the 15% zone, and this combination just meets that requirement. The 8-lamination beam, on the other hand, requires 1.2 laminations of depth for the 15% outer zones, and the two laminations exceed this requirement. The 8-lamination glulam combination results in 25% outer zones and would be expected to have slightly higher strength and stiffness than the 13-lamination beam.

An ASTM D 3737 analysis of this glulam combination utilizing 1.4E lumber in 15% of the outer zones resulted in a design glulam MOE value of 1.2×10^6 lb/in^2. This design value was governed by the analytical results of the critical 13-lamination beam. The calculated design bending strength, which was also governed by the 13-lamination beam, was

Table 4—Estimated properties of ponderosa pine laminating grades for ASTM D 3737 analysis

Grade	MOE ($\times 10^6$ lb/in^2)	Mean knot size[a] (%)	99.5% knot size[b] (%)	Minimum bending strength ratio	Bending stress index (lb/in^2)
Provided by AITC					
1.6E–1/4EK	1.6	10.3	48.9	0.65	2,560
1.4E–1/4EK	1.4	10.6	51.8	0.65	2,100
1.2E–1/4EK	1.2	11.4	60.0	0.65	1,650
No. 2	1.0	11.5	56.8	0.45	1,800
Developed by FPL					
1.4E–1/2EK	1.4	12.0	60.0	0.50	2,100

[a]Average of sum of all knot sizes within each 1-ft length, taken at 0.1-ft intervals (ASTM 2000a).
[b]99.5 percentile knot size (ASTM 2000a).

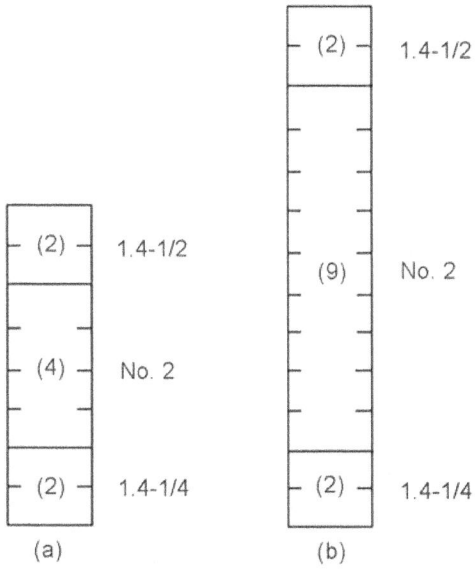

Figure 2—Ponderosa pine glulam combinations:
(a) 8-lamination and (b) 13-lamination.

Figure 3—Standard and Better grade ponderosa pine
lumber. Approximately 36% of pieces have pith-
associated wood.

Figure 4—Continuous lumber tester used to test
lumber for MOE. Panels removed to show rollers.

1,250 lb/in^2. This value is based on the 302–20 grade (AITC
2004) of tension lamination used in the bottom lamination.
When a tension lamination is not used, as targeted in this
study, the design bending strength is 1,050 lb/in^2 for beams
≤15 in. deep and 950 lb/in^2 for beams >15 in. deep. These
are standard 15% and 25% reductions, respectively, for the
two ranges of beam depth.

Material and Methods

This section describes the procedures taken to characterize
the properties of the laminating lumber as well as the fabri-
cation of the experimental glulam beams.

The ponderosa pine lumber was harvested from the Apache–
Sitgreaves National Forest of eastern Arizona. The lumber
was Standard and Better grade kiln-dried and surfaced on
four sides (WWPA 2000). Unique to this lumber set is that
the majority was processed from small-diameter timber. As a
result, a significant number of pieces had pith-associated
wood, or juvenile wood, in the cross section.

Figure 3 shows a typical bundle of Standard and Better
grade lumber prior to mechanical grading and sorting; pieces
that contained juvenile wood in the cross section are apparent. More than 36% of this lumber contained juvenile wood.
Because juvenile wood is defined as approximately the first
20 to 25 years of growth, the amount of lumber having a
large percentage of juvenile wood would actually be larger
than 36%. We also observed considerable warp in this lumber as well as a significant release of stress when the lumber
straps were cut from the bundles.

The 7,972 pieces of lumber individually marked with a
unique identification number and then processed through a
continuous lumber tester (CLT) (Metriguard, Inc., Pullman,
Washington) (Fig. 4). Lumber was processed through the
CLT through a series of rollers at approximately 200 ft/min.
The rollers are spaced so as to create two continuous 48-in.
spans. A fixed displacement is applied at the center of each
span (an upward displacement and a downward displacement). The resultant loads in each span are measured at 1-in.
increments, which provides the information necessary for
determining MOE. This information, which is stored in a
computer text file, includes the average of all MOE values
along the length of the member, the low-point MOE value,
and the location of the low-point MOE value.

The CLT software was set so that different color sprays were
used for different ranges of lumber MOE (Table 5). The
ranges targeted an average MOE level that matched those
values targeted for the experimental beam combination

Table 5—CLT software settings for sorting various MOE groups

Group number	Minimum MOE (10^6 lb/in^2)	Maximum MOE (10^6 lb/in^2)	Spray color
1	1.70	>1.70	Orange
2	1.10	1.69	Green
3	0.80	1.09	Purple
4	<0.80	0.79	None

(Fig. 2), along with a low-MOE grade (average 1.0×10^6 lb/in^2).

Specimens in groups 1 and 4 (Table 5) were removed to avoid any unusually high or low MOE values in the targeted mechanical grades. Group 2 specimens were targeted for 1.4E lumber and group 3 specimens for 1.0E lumber (for use in a future study to establish a low-MOE E-rated lumber grade). Information from the CLT, which was stored in an ASCII text file, included lumber length, average MOE, low-point MOE, location of low-point MOE, and corresponding group number. The calculated MOE values were based on the 1.5- by 3.5-in. cross-sectional dimensions of the lumber.

Immediately after testing, each piece of lumber was visually graded to determine if it met laminating stock criteria (wane, skip, and/or warp) and for sorting into the targeted 1/4- or 1/2-edge knot grades (Fig. 5). Once all the lumber needed for the outer lamination grades was gathered, pieces for the core laminations were gathered from the unsorted Standard and Better grade lumber. The Standard and Better grade lumber was processed through the CLT machine to record information on MOE. The material was visually graded to ensure that it met No. 2 grade requirements and laminating requirements (wane, skip, and/or warp).

Finally, a static deflection test was conducted to determine MOE. The test measured deflection caused by a 10-lb weight on the full span of specimens in the flatwise orientation. A significant number of these specimens were targeted in each sorted lumber group to develop a relationship between CLT MOE and static MOE throughout the full range of MOE values. It was necessary to develop this relationship because it verified the proper calibration of the CLT machine and provided static MOE values as specified in ASTM D 3737 (ASTM 2000a).

Lumber Grading

Table 6 shows the CLT MOE results of all 7,972 pieces of lumber processed through the CLT machine. This total also includes lumber that did not meet laminating grade visual criteria, such as wane, skip, and/or warp. As Table 6 shows, 3,403 pieces of group 2 (42.7%) met the targeted 1.4E grade

Figure 5—Grading of lumber: (top) visual grading of lumber after exiting CLT machine; (bottom) bundles of lumber sorted by MOE and visual lumber grade.

Table 6—CLT MOE results for ponderosa pine lumber[a]

Group[b]	Sample size	MOE test results[c] Average (10^6 lb/in^2)	MOE test results[c] COV (%)	Low point to avg MOE Ratio	Low point to avg MOE COV (%)
All	7,972	1.166	28.5	0.713	21.3
1	556	1.850	6.6	0.821	11.3
2	3,403	1.356	12.0	0.774	11.5
3	1,335	0.997	8.0	0.789	8.2
4	2,678	0.867	23.4	0.577	27.9

[a]Standard and Better grade.
[b]Group numbers correspond to those defined in Table 2.
[c]COV is coefficient of variation.

and 1,335 pieces of group 3 (16.7%) the targeted 1.0E grade. The total number of pieces meeting these two MOE levels was 59.4%. In normal production, group 1 specimens would also be included in beam manufacture, which would result in approximately 66.4% of pieces meeting or exceeding the targeted MOE levels of 1.0E and 1.4E.

Approximately 1,090 pieces were used in beam manufacture, 181 pieces were processed into finger-jointed lumber specimens for testing, and 973 pieces remained as solid-sawn lumber for testing. Of the total of 7,972 pieces, 2,244 pieces met laminating stock criteria, which is approximately 28.1% yield. Wane and skip were the primary controlling factors for the high rate of rejection of lumber for laminating stock from this Standard and Better grade lumber. If this lumber had been processed at the sawmill to a slightly thicker green dimension so that the final dressed size would have had fewer pieces with wane and skip, our yield of laminating stock would have been much higher than 28.1%. Another option that would have solved this problem would have been to re-plane the lumber during glulam manufacture.

The mechanical properties of the lumber are the most important aspect of this grading process. We determined that 66% of the Standard and Better grade resource possessed the properties suitable for glulam manufacture. This yield was not fully realized because of the large quantity of lumber rejected because of wane and skip.

Finally, to verify the validity of the CLT results, a total of 221 lumber specimens were tested for flatwise static MOE. These specimens were sampled throughout a wide range of MOE values to develop a regression relationship between CLT MOE and static MOE (Fig. 6). The regression relationship shown in Figure 6 had a very high coefficient of determination (r^2) of 0.983. Because the difference in magnitude of the two MOE values was very small (within 3.6% at 1.0E and within 1.5% at 1.4E), no adjustments to the CLT MOE values were made in subsequent analyses. The small differences between CLT MOE and long-span static MOE were not large enough to affect the ASTM D 245 (ASTM 2000c) rounding rules for lumber MOE.

Glulam Beam Manufacture

The initial step of glulam manufacture involved finger-jointing the lumber end-to-end. The standard (1.113-in.-long) finger-joint profile was used. The order of manufacture was first finger jointing of the 1.4E–1/2EK grade laminations, then the core laminations, and finally the 1.4E–1/4EK grade laminations. These laminations were dry-stacked with the compression laminations on the bottom (1.4E–1/2EK) and tension laminations on the top (1.4E–1/4EK) (Fig. 7).

The 8-lamination beams were processed as 48-ft-long members and the 13-lamination beams as 64-ft-long members. The lumber ID number and the location of the finger joints were recorded during dry-stacking of the full-length laminations. This mapping procedure allowed the recording of lumber placement in the experimental glulam beams, which will provide valuable data for future analyses. Appendix A contains the actual beam maps for all the glulam beams tested in this study, along with the MOE properties of the lumber.

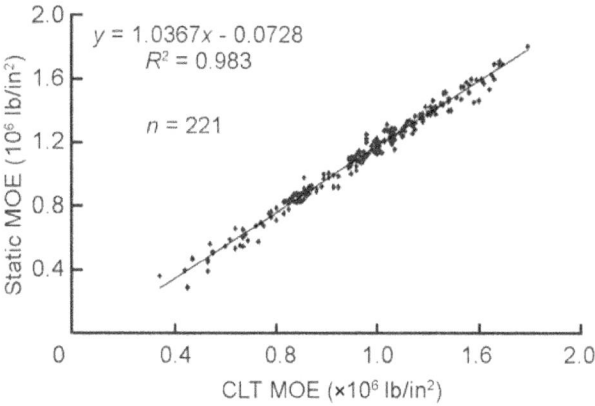

Figure 6—Regression relationship between static MOE and CLT MOE of ponderosa pine laminating lumber.

Figure 7—Dry stacking of finger-jointed laminating lumber. Note lumber, lamination, and beam identification numbers.

Properties of Laminating Lumber

The MOE properties were obtained from the lumber that was actually mapped within the beams. Knot properties for conducting an ASTM D 3737 analysis were determined from measurements taken on graded lumber that was sampled for laboratory testing. These lumber grades were sampled during glulam beam manufacture and were representative of the lumber used in the beams. A summary of the knot analysis is included in Appendix B. Moisture contents were measured at the laminating plant throughout the duration of the manufacturing process. The lumber was determined to have an average moisture content of 8.8%, with a range of 7% to 12%. Table 7 shows the results of MOE for the lumber mapped within the beams and for the lumber sampled for laboratory testing. Results on knot properties were based on the lumber sampled for laboratory testing.

Table 7—Summary of actual lumber MOE and knot properties[a]

| Grade | Lumber MOE | | | Knot properties[b] | | |
	Sample size	Average ($\times 10^6$ lb/in^2)	COV (%)	Lineal footage (ft)	x-bar (%)	h (%)
Lumber mapped in glulam beams						
1.4E–1/4EK	344	1.343	11.5	—	—	—
1.4E–1/2EK	340	1.309	12.7	—	—	—
Core	999	1.109	27.6	—	—	—
Lumber sampled for laboratory tests						
1.4E–1/4EK	121	1.232	14.7	525	11.0	42.7
1.4E–1/2EK	144	1.209	17.0	534	15.9	47.4
1.0E–1/4EK	108	0.984	8.2	508	11.2	40.0
1.0E–1/2EK	364	0.994	10.3	1,020	13.3	50.0
All 1/4EK grade	—	—	—	1,033	11.1	41.3
All 1/2EK grade	—	—	—	1,554	14.2	48.7

[a]To adjust lumber MOE values to 100:1 span-to-depth static MOE value, use the following relationship:
$y = 1.0367x - 0.0728$.
[b]x-bar is mean knot size; h is difference between 99.5th percentile knot size and mean knot size (ASTM 2000a).

The resulting average MOE values of the lumber actually mapped in the beams shows that the targeted MOE level of 1.4×10^6 lb/in^2 was not achieved for the two grades of 1.4E lumber. The 1.4E lumber mapped in the glulam beams only achieved a 1.3E level, and the lumber sampled for laboratory testing only achieved a 1.2E level. As for the 1.0E grade, we found that the targeted MOE levels were exactly met, with resulting average MOE values of 0.98×10^6 lb/in^2 and 0.99×10^6 lb/in^2 for the 1.0E–1/4EK and 1.0E–1/2EK grades, respectively.

Properties of Solid-Sawn and Finger-Jointed Lumber

To relate lumber properties to glulam properties, the mechanical properties of matched samples of laminating lumber for each grade used in the glulam combinations were evaluated. The predominantly 12-ft-long lumber was sorted into two primary groups matched by lumber MOE: specimens to be tested in tension and those to be tested in edgewise bending. After processing an approximately 7-ft-long specimen from each 12-ft piece of lumber, additional test specimens were cut from the remaining 5-ft-long piece of lumber. These additional specimens included an approximately 3-ft-long specimen for flatwise bending and a short specimen for the standard notched shear block test. With this cutting scheme, we obtained matched samples of tensile strength and edgewise bending properties, and all specimens had lumber MOE, flatwise bending, and shear strength properties. The presence of strength-reducing defects in the tension and bending specimens was allowed to occur randomly.

As Table 7 indicates, average MOE values of the lumber sampled for laboratory testing did not accurately match average MOE values of the lumber mapped in the glulam members. Consequently, we sorted the laboratory-tested lumber so that its average MOE properties matched those reported for the glulam beams and are reported in Table 8. These sorted MOE properties closely approximated the mapped beam MOE properties. The corresponding strength properties for those matched lumber groups were characterized and reported in Table 9. This method of sorting assured that the distributions of lumber properties characterized in Tables 8 and 9 were representative of the lumber grades mapped in the glulam members (Table 7). This characterization will be critical in future research involving glulam modeling.

In addition to tests on solid-sawn lumber, finger-jointed lumber specimens were tested in tension. This test was conducted to evaluate the ANSI A190.1 requirement that the 5th percentile tensile strength of the bottom lamination in finger-joint grade must achieve a level 1.67 times the design bending strength of a glulam beam. Figure 8 shows the distribution of tensile strength of 1.4E–1/4EK grade finger-jointed lumber specimens. As is common with lower strength lumber, a significant number of failures were observed to occur away from the finger joint, usually in a strength-reducing defect such as a knot. Only 18 of 41 specimens in the 1.4E grade failed at the finger joint.

The lowest ranking tensile strength of a specimen with a finger-joint failure was 1,690 lb/in^2, which would serve as

Table 8—Best-fitting distributions of flatwise lumber MOE for each glulam beam group[a]

| Beam group | Lumber grade | Best-fit distribution | Sample size | Distribution parameter[b] | | | Mean ($\times 10^6$ lb/in^2) | COV (%) | 5th percentile ($\times 10^6$ lb/in^2) |
				Location	Scale	Shape			
8-Lam F_{bx}	1.4–1/4	3-P Lognormal	88	0.7289	–0.5096	0.2742	1.3526	27.9	1.0991
	1.4–1/2	3-P Weibull	75	0.4231	0.8783	2.3092	1.2326	14.2	0.9264
	Core	2-P Lognormal	167	0.0000	–0.0319	0.2767	1.0064	28.2	0.6002
8-Lam F_{bt}	1.4–1/4	3-P Weibull	46	1.0967	0.2471	1.2732	1.3180	10.6	1.1363
	1.4–1/2	2-P Lognormal	61	0.0000	0.2241	0.1277	1.2614	12.8	0.9949
	Core	2-P Lognormal	101	0.0000	–0.0418	0.2436	0.9879	24.7	0.6250
8-Lam all	1.4–1/4	3-P Lognormal	134	0.7492	–0.5614	0.2716	1.3411	27.7	1.1047
	1.4–1/2	3-P Weibull	136	0.2893	1.0312	2.5081	1.2485	14.3	0.9324
	Core	2-P Lognormal	268	0.0000	–0.0357	0.2647	0.9994	26.9	0.6135
13-Lam F_{bx}	1.4–1/4	2-P Lognormal	112	0.0000	0.2884	0.1223	1.3443	12.3	1.0769
	1.4–1/2	3-P Weibull	97	1.0999	0.2573	1.3489	1.3286	9.8	1.1502
	Core	3-P Weibull	471	0.5099	0.6976	1.4336	1.1279	27.9	0.6744
13-Lam F_{by}	1.4–1/4	2-P Lognormal	41	0.0000	0.2977	0.1054	1.3543	10.6	1.1101
	1.4–1/2	3-P Lognormal	48	1.0933	–1.4967	0.7457	1.3890	86.2	1.1510
	Core	2-P Lognormal	204	0.0000	0.1042	0.2764	1.1531	28.2	0.6894
13-Lam F_{vx}	1.4–1/4	3-P Lognormal	57	0.8778	–0.8382	0.3804	1.3427	39.5	1.0956
	1.4–1/2	3-P Weibull	59	1.0964	0.2900	1.3333	1.3545	11.1	1.1510
	Core	3-P Weibull	247	0.2763	1.0094	1.7748	1.1797	26.6	0.6694
13-Lam all	1.4–1/4	2-P Lognormal	210	0.0000	0.2893	0.1167	1.3446	11.7	1.0925
	1.4–1/2	3-P Weibull	204	1.0985	0.2768	1.3406	1.3446	10.5	1.1515
	Core	3-P Weibull	922	0.3910	0.8534	1.6277	1.1495	26.8	0.6692
	1.4–1/4	2-P Lognormal	344	0.0000	0.2880	0.1148	1.3426	11.5	1.1445
All	1.4–1/2	2-P Lognormal	340	0.0000	0.2614	0.1269	1.3092	12.7	1.0965
	Core	3-P Weibull	1,190	0.3595	0.8429	1.6217	1.1085	27.6	0.6319

[a]To adjust lumber MOE values to 100:1 span-to-depth static MOE value, use the following relationship:
$y = 1.0367x - 0.0728$.
[b]For lognormal, scale = average of LN(x) and shape = standard deviation of LN(x).

the non-parametric 5th percentile. The 50th percentile value, with all failures included, was 3,266 lb/in^2. If the ANSI A190.1 qualification stress level factor of 1.67 were applied to the non-parametric 5th percentile value, the corresponding glulam design bending strength for which these finger joints would qualify would be 1,012 lb/in^2. Figure 9 shows the cumulative distribution of tensile strength for the 1.0E grade finger-jointed lumber specimens. The 50th percentile value, with all failures included, was 2,507 lb/in^2, and the lowest ranking finger-joint tensile strength was 1,313 lb/in^2. These 1.0E finger-jointed lumber specimens were representative of the finger joints that occur in the core laminations of the glulam test specimens.

Loading Configurations and Data Acquisition

Four types of glulam tests were conducted: edgewise bending, flatwise bending, beam shear, and beam tension. Figures 10 and 11 show a 13-lamination beam during edgewise and flatwise bending, respectively. Figures 12 and 13 show a 13-lamination glulam beam during shear and tension tests, respectively. Table 10 provides information on test spans and data acquisition. The targeted time-to-failure for all glulam beam and lumber tests was 10 min, with all failures occurring between 5 and 20 min as specified in ASTM standard D 198 (ASTM 2000b).

Table 9—Best-fitting distributions of solid-sawn lumber strength for each glulam beam group

| Lumber grade | Best-fit distribution | Sample size | Distribution parameter[a] | | | Mean (lb/in²) | COV (%) | 5th percentile (lb/in²) |
			Location	Scale	Shape			
			Flatwise lumber modulus of rupture					
1.4–1/4	3-P Weibull	25	2815.7	5578.6	3.6182	7843.9	19.7	5270.4
1.4–1/2	2-P Lognormal	67	0.0000	8.8967	0.2275	7499.4	23.0	4869.2
Core	2-P Lognormal	51	0.0000	8.7837	0.2764	6781.0	28.2	3956.5
			Lumber ultimate tensile strength					
1.4–1/4	2-P Lognormal	12	0.0000	8.2324	0.2630	3893.3	26.8	2194.7
1.4–1/2	2-P Lognormal	46	0.0000	8.0718	0.3191	3370.2	32.7	1790.8
Core	2-P Lognormal	43	0.0000	7.9258	0.2830	2880.9	28.9	1649.1
			Edgewise lumber modulus of rupture					
1.4–1/4	2-P Lognormal	24	0.0000	8.7837	0.3557	6953.2	36.7	3319.0
1.4–1/2	2-P Lognormal	34	0.0000	8.5546	0.2503	5356.0	25.4	3267.0
Core	2-P Lognormal	26	0.0000	8.4040	0.2450	4600.7	24.9	2807.3
			ASTM shear block strength					
1.4–1/4	2-P Lognormal	23	0.0000	6.8459	0.1389	949.09	14.0	721.10
1.4–1/2	2-P Lognormal	67	0.0000	6.8556	0.1099	954.95	11.0	780.13
Core	3-P Weibull	47	654.70	248.05	2.0519	874.45	12.8	713.03

[a]For lognormal, scale is average of LN(x) and shape is standard deviation of LN(x).

Edgewise Bending Tests

Edgewise bending tests (Fig. 10) were conducted on both the 8- and 13-lamination glulam combinations. Sixteen beams of each configuration were tested (15 test beams plus 1 beam with high MOE outer laminations). The glulam beams were supported on rocker-type platforms that pivoted as the beams deflected as a result of loading; this type of support allows minor translation during loading. Lateral roller supports were used at intervals along the beam length to prevent lateral torsional buckling. Force was applied with a loading beam having two attached loading points that were also capable of pivoting as the beam increased in curvature. The support span was set at a 21:1 span-to-depth ratio, according to ASTM D 198 (ASTM 2000b). To reduce the possibility of local crushing, thick maple blocks were used between the load points and the beam surface to increase the area of contact. The distance between the load points was 20% of the support span. The trapezoidal moment diagram created with this loading configuration approximated the parabolic moment diagram created by a uniform load configuration.

Load was measured using a 250,000-lb capacity load cell above the loading beam. Long-span center-point deflection was measured using a linear variable displacement transducer (LVDT) attached to a piano wire strung tightly at the neutral axis between the two supports. The LVDT had a 6-in. maximum gauge length, and the resolution was 0.005 in. Shear-free deflection was measured across a shorter span between the two load points. A tripod-type yoke was used to hold the LVDT in place during measurement of deflection caused by increasing the curvature of the top surface of the beam. The LVDT had a 1-in. maximum gauge length, and the resolution was 0.001 in.

Flatwise Bending Tests

Flatwise bending tests (Fig. 11) were conducted on only the 13-lamination beams. This setup required wider rocker supports and loading point blocks than the edgewise tests so that a line load could be applied across the entire width of the beam. Long-span deflection was measured with respect to the load head, and no shear-free deflection measurements were taken. Support span was also set to a 21:1 span-to-depth ratio; however, in this case, the depth was the beam width. Distance between the load points was also set to 20% of the support span.

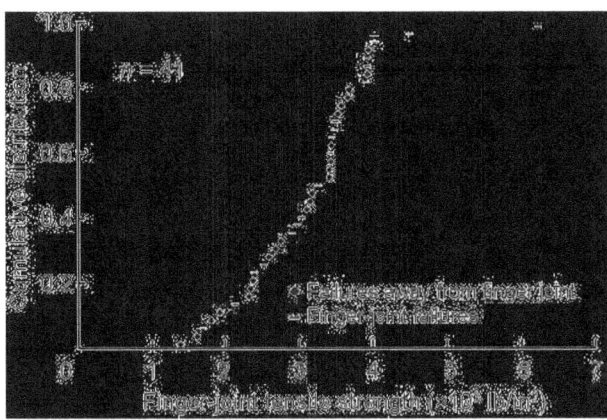

Figure 8—Cumulative distribution of tensile strength of 1.4E grade finger-jointed lumber specimens.

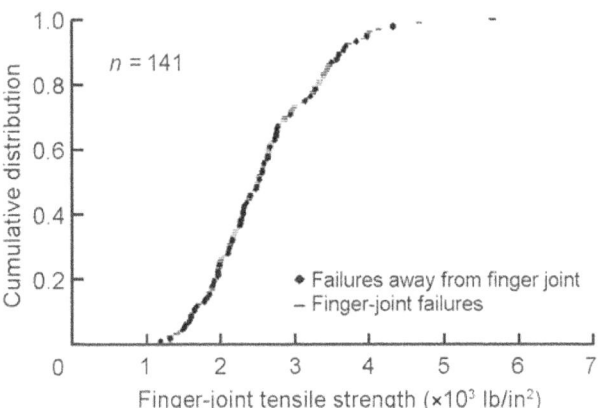

Figure 9—Cumulative distribution of tensile strength of 1.0E grade finger-jointed lumber specimens.

Figure 10—Edgewise bending test of 13-lamination glulam beam.

Figure 11—Testing of 13-lamination glulam beam: (top) flatwise bending test; (bottom) LVDT placement for measuring center-span deflection.

Edgewise Shear Tests

Only the 13-lamination glulam beams were tested for shear strength (Fig. 12) using a bending test setup with a shorter span than that used for the other tests. The loading configuration used a span-to-depth ratio of 6:0 with a symmetric two-point loading configuration, as recommended by Yeh (1997). Two loading points were used so that localized crushing would not occur under a single load-point; however, the loading points were spaced close together so that the test setup would closely simulate a center-point-loaded configuration. Although not necessary for development of design values, we measured the full-span deflection of these beams with respect to the neutral axis. These data, along with long-span and shear-free deflections measured on other beams, will provide useful information on the effect of shear deformation when modeling glulam MOE using lumber MOE values.

Tension Tests

Unique to this study was the utilization of a large-capacity tension machine (Fig. 13), with a 200,000-lb load cell, to

Figure 12—Glulam beam shear tests: (top) end view of support block, stringline for measuring deflection, and lateral supports; (bottom) close-up of load points and radiused contact blocks.

Figure 13—Testing of 8-lamination glulam beam: (top) tension test; (bottom) close-up of tension grips.

The tension grips had a pinned connection at each end to ensure that no bending moment was exerted on the members.

Results

Inspection of the test beams revealed that one beam designated for edgewise bending had a very large center knot in the bottom lamination near a finger joint. The ANSI A190.1 standard (ANSI/AITC 2004) states that knots of this size cannot occur within two knot-diameters from a finger joint located in the maximum moment regions of a glulam beam. For this reason, this beam was excluded from the test group and from all analyses. Table 11 summarizes the results of the glulam strength and stiffness tests. Details of glulam beam tests are provided in Appendix C.

Edgewise Bending

All glulam beam failures exhibited linear load–deflection behavior up to the ultimate load, with failure primarily due to knots and pith-associated wood in the outer two tension laminations. The results in Table 11 show that the average

evaluate the 8-lamination glulam members in tension. A 1-in.-long gauge LVDT with 0.001-in. resolution and an aluminum rod were pinned to the side of the member to measure axial displacement over a 96-in. gauge length. The distance between the tension grips was 152 in. Hydraulic pressure to the tension grips was increased as the tensile load increased, so that no slipping would occur during the test.

Table 10—Summary of loading configurations used in glulam beam tests

Beam group[a]	Properties tested[b]	Orientation	Support span (in.)	Load span (in.)
8-Lam F_{bx}	MOR_x, E_x, E_{sf}[c]	Edgewise	253	50
13-Lam F_{bx}	MOR_x, E_x, E_{sf}[c]	Edgewise	408	82
13-Lam F_{by}	MOR_y, E_y	Flatwise	65.8	13.1
13-Lam F_{vx}	$Shear_x$, E_x	Edgewise	117	14
8-Lam F_t	UTS, E_{axial}	Axial[d]	152	96

[a] F_{bx} refers to horizontally laminated bending, F_{by} vertically laminated bending, F_{vx} horizontally laminated shear, and F_t tension.
[b] MOR is modulus of rupture, E modulus of elasticity, and UTS ultimate tensile strength.
[c] Shear-free deflection was measured on 32-in. span for 8-lamination beams and 56-in. span for 13-lamination beams.
[d] For axial tests, support span value was distance between grips; load span value was gauge length of aluminum rod.

MOR of the 8-lamination combination was 6.3% higher and the apparent MOE 4.3% higher than that of the 13-lamination combination. This difference in strength performance can be attributed to volume effect. However, note that the 13-lamination beam consisted of 70% No. 2 grade core laminations, whereas the 8-lamination beam had only 50% No. 2 grade core laminations by design. The higher percentage of high-grade laminations in the 8-lamination beam would also explain its higher stiffness performance.

The glulam MOR test results for both beam combinations were plotted in the form of cumulative distribution plots (Fig. 14). The plots show, as expected, that the average MOR of the 8-lamination beam was higher than that of the 13-lamination beam.

Volume Effect

One objective in evaluating two beam sizes was to verify that existing industry standards for the volume effect were applicable to these ponderosa pine glulam beams. The volume effect equation for glulam has the form

$$C_v = \left(\frac{12}{d}\right)^{1/x} \left(\frac{5.125}{w}\right)^{1/y} \left(\frac{21}{L}\right)^{1/z} \qquad (1)$$

where
C_v is volume effect factor,
d beam depth (in.),
w beam width (in.), and
L beam length (ft), and
x,y,z are exponents for depth, width, and length, respectively.

In current glulam standards, x, y, and z are assigned a value of 20 for Southern Pine and 10 for all other species. Glulam beam data are adjusted to a standard size beam (5.125 in. wide, 12 in. deep, 21 ft long). The volume effect exponent for our set of ponderosa pine glulam beams was calculated by transforming the raw data into exponential space and performing a simple linear regression analysis on the transformed data. The volume effect exponent was calculated using all the beams ($n = 29$), and this value was found to be equal to 0.062, which corresponds to an x, y, and z value of 16 for Equation (1). Using the industry standard 0.10 volume

Table 11—Strength and MOE results for flexure, shear, and tension tests of ponderosa pine glulam[a]

Group	Sample size	Lognormal distribution Avg (lb/in²)	COV (%)	Normal distribution Avg (lb/in²)	COV (%)	Apparent MOE Avg (×10⁶ lb/in²)	COV (%)	Shear-free MOE Avg (×10⁶ lb/in²)	COV (%)
8-Lam F_{bx}	15	4,560	17.4	4,560	17.3	1.373	5.8	1.508	11.9
13-Lam F_{bx}	14	4,290	16.7	4,290	16.7	1.316	4.7	1.414	8.0
13-Lam F_{by}	15	5,720	13.9	5,710	13.8	1.263	7.7	–	–
13-Lam F_{vx}	16	357	33.5	354	28.4	1.047	8.6	–	–
8-Lam F_t	15	3,040	14.9	3,040	15.4	1.344	8.2	–	–

[a] No adjustments were made to data; results include all failure modes.
For F_{bx} and F_{by} groups, strength results are modulus of rupture; for F_{vx} group, shear strength; for F_t group, tensile strength. For F_{bx}, F_{by}, and F_{vx} groups, stiffness results are bending modulus of elasticity; for F_t group, tensile modulus of elasticity. F_{vx} group MOE was based on short-span bending test and was heavily influenced by shear deformation.

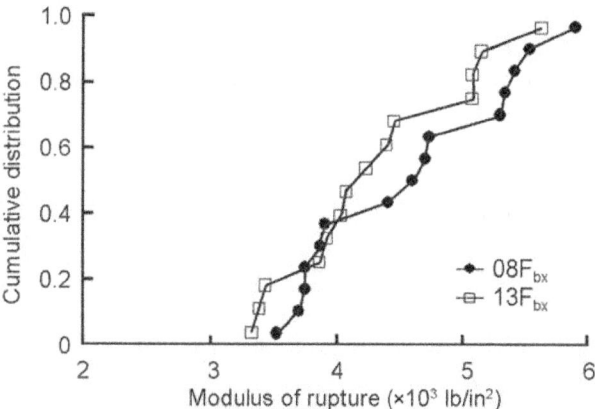

Figure 14—Cumulative distribution plots of 8- and 13-lamination glulam beams (all data).

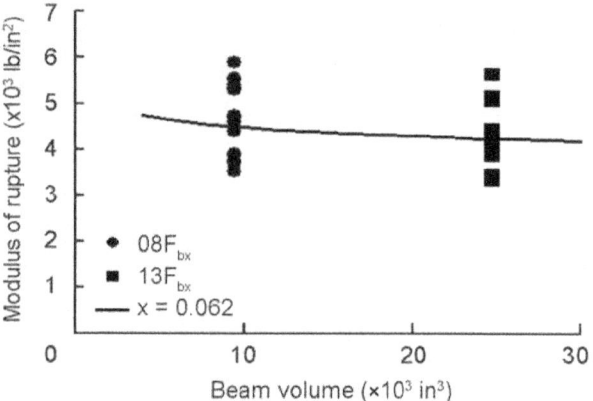

Figure 15—Calculated MOE as a function of beam volume.

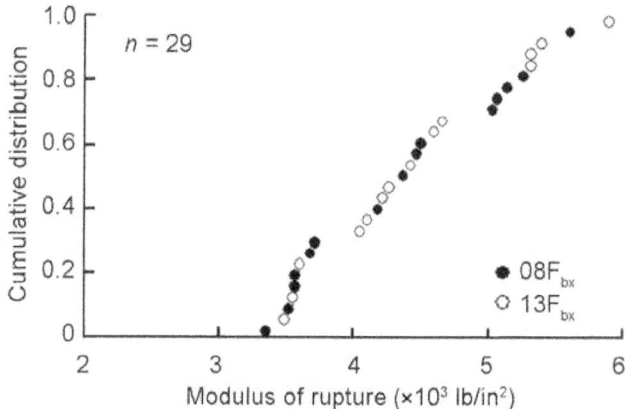

Figure 16—Cumulative distribution of edgewise glulam MOR, adjusted to standard beam dimensions.

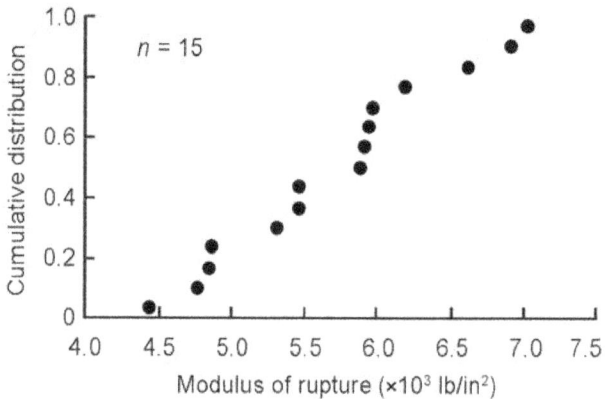

Figure 17—Cumulative distribution of flatwise glulam MOR (vertically laminated members).

effect exponent, the two glulam data sets were adjusted to a standard size glulam beam. A two-sample t-test determined that the means of the two distributions of adjusted MOR were statistically equal. This confirmed that the 8- and 13-lamination beam data could be combined, after adjustment for the volume effect, and justified the use of the 0.10 volume effect exponent. Figure 15 shows raw MOR data plotted as a function of beam volume.

The beam data for both groups were adjusted to a standard beam 5.125 in. wide, 12 in. deep, and 21 ft long. The data were plotted in Figure 16 in the form of a cumulative distribution.

Flatwise Bending

The flatwise bending specimens exhibited linear load–deflection behavior up to initial failure. Initial failure always occurred in the outer two E-rated laminations on each side of the beam at a strength-controlling knot. A brief reduction in load was observed after initial failure, and then the load

would increase again at a slightly lower load–deflection slope. No visible crushing was observed at the supports or loading points, and maximum load was used for bending strength calculations. Figure 17 shows a cumulative distribution plot of all 15 beam test results.

The results in Table 11 show that the calculated MOR value of flatwise bending specimens (vertically laminated) were significantly higher than those of edgewise bending specimens (horizontally laminated). This is the opposite of what is commonly found in AITC 117 design (AITC 2004), where vertically laminated combinations typically have lower design values for F_{by}. The F_{by} values are typically lower than the F_{bx} values for bending combinations, because the methodology used to calculate allowable bending strength is governed by the lower-grade core laminations.

Based on the lognormal distribution, average MOR was 5,720 lb/in^2 for the flatwise bending specimens and 4,170 lb/in^2 for the edgewise bending specimens. At the 5th percentile (75% tolerance), the flatwise bending specimens had an MOR of 4,130 lb/in^2 and the edgewise bending specimens an MOR of 2,380 lb/in^2. These results show that the ratio of flatwise to edgewise MOR was 1.37 at the average and 1.74 at the 5th percentile. By comparison, the F_{bx} to F_{by} ratio in AITC 117 (AITC 2004) is 0.66 for the 16F–E1 combination and 0.55 for the 20F–E1 combination. Both of these combinations were made using Softwood species. In conclusion, the results show that the relative performance of vertically and horizontally laminated beams was much higher than what is usually published in existing standards. Our results indicate that allowing the low-grade core laminations to govern the allowable F_{by} properties of a bending combination is conservative.

Edgewise Shear

The edgewise shear specimens (F_{vx}) exhibited linear load–deflection behavior up to failure. The short-span loading configuration was designed so that the majority of members would fail in horizontal shear through the inner laminations. However, some bending failures were still expected with this loading configuration, due to the strength-reducing defects present in the outer laminations of the tension zone. In this study, 9 of 16 beams tested had initial failures as a result of shear (Fig. 18); the remaining 7 beams had initial failure as a result of bending stress in the tension zone.

Figure 18 shows good overlap of bending and shear failures throughout the shear stress distribution. In general, the majority of shear failures (5 of 8) occurred in the lower half of the distribution and failures were equally distributed (4 of 8) in the upper half. This mixture of failure types required a censored-data analysis to accurately calculate the characteristic shear stress values of only those beams failing in shear. The calculated shear strength results based on a censored data analysis of all 16 beams were as follows:

Lognormal distribution			Normal distribution		
Avg	COV	5th$_{0.75}$ percentile	Avg	COV	5th$_{0.75}$ percentile
525 lb/in^2	21.5%	156 lb/in^2	403 lb/in^2	33.1%	143 lb/in^2

Thus, all 16 data values were used in the censored analysis, and shear properties were based on 9 shear failures and 7 censored points. The results were based on the calculated correlation between shear and bending, assuming that the shear/bending pairs had a bivariate normal distribution. For the lognormal case, the shear/bending pairs were assumed to have a bivariate normal distribution after the logs were taken.

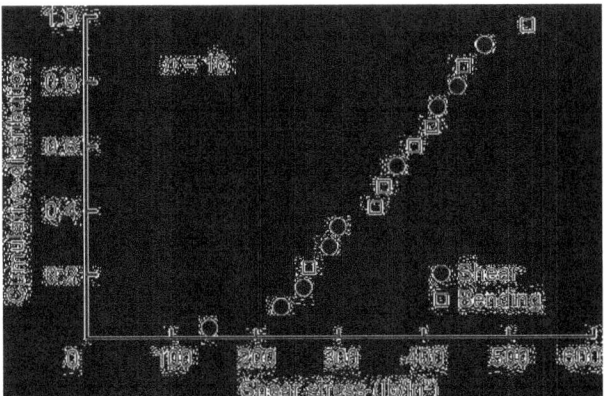

Figure 18—Cumulative distribution of glulam edgewise shear.

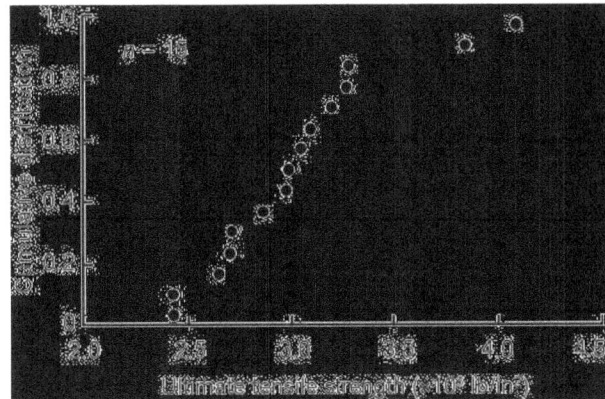

Figure 19—Cumulative distribution of glulam tensile strength.

Tension

The axial tension specimens exhibited linear load–deflection behavior, with ultimate failure occurring abruptly. Significant cracking usually began at about 50% of ultimate load; however, no visible failures were seen until ultimate failure. Failures were observed to follow a path of least resistance from strength-reducing defects in one lamination to the next; failures were primarily observed at knots and pith-associated wood. Figure 19 is a cumulative distribution plot of all 15 tension test results.

Modulus of Elasticity

For edgewise bending (MOE$_x$), the design glulam MOE level was 1.2×10^6 lb/in^2, based on the assumed properties of Table 4 and taking 95% of the MOE calculated by a transformed section analysis (ASTM 2004a). The average glulam MOE results calculated from beam tests were 1.373 and 1.313×10^6 lb/in^2 for the 8- and 13-lamination beams, respectively. For the members tested in flatwise bending, the calculated design MOE value was 1.07×10^6 lb/in^2, based on

Table 4 lumber properties and taking 95% of the average lumber MOE of all laminations (ASTM 2000a). The average MOE values calculated from beam tests was 1.263×10^6 lb/in^2 for the 13-lamination flatwise members. For the axially loaded members, the calculated design MOE value was 1.12×10^6 lb/in^2, based on Table 4 lumber properties and taking the weighted average lumber MOE of all laminations (ASTM 2000a). The average glulam axial MOE was 1.344×10^6 lb/in^2 for the 8-lamination beams. In all instances, the experimental beam test results exceeded the calculated design levels based on design lumber MOE properties. Note that the 8-lamination glulam combination had slightly higher MOE values in all cases as a result of the larger percentage of higher-MOE outer laminations.

In this study, shear-free deflections were also measured on the edgewise bending members, which allowed comparison of the two types of calculated MOE values. The U.S. standards for glulam are based on long-span deflections and the international glulam standards on shear-free deflections. For the 8- and 13-lamination beam combinations, the calculated shear-free MOE values were respectively 9.8% and 7.6% higher than the calculated long-span MOE values. This relationship is important to understand because it shows that the same beam combination can have two different reported MOE values, based on the type of deflection that is measured.

Analysis

Glulam Design Values

In this section, we describe the procedures used to calculate the allowable design values for each mechanical property of glulam. For all strength properties, the allowable design values are based on the calculated 5th percentile of the strength distribution. The allowable design strength values for bending, tension, and shear were calculated using the following equation:

$$F = (5th_{0.75})/2.1 \qquad (2)$$

where F is calculated design strength value, $5th_{0.75}$ is 5th percentile strength value at 75% tolerance, and 2.1 is a factor that includes adjustment for safety and duration of load. For glulam MOE, the allowable design value is the average of the apparent MOE distribution, as reported in Table 11.

Edgewise Bending Strength (F_{bx})

The 5th percentile (at 75% tolerance) edgewise MOR was calculated from the combined data (adjusted for volume effect) shown in Figure 16, which resulted in a value of 3,020 lb/in^2. The allowable design bending strength F_{bx} was determined to be 1,440 lb/in^2. As previously mentioned, the only all ponderosa pine glulam combination in existing standards that could be made with this resource is the homo-

geneous L3 combination, which has an F_{bx} value of 850 lb/in^2. Thus, through mechanical grading of the outer lamination grades, a new combination was developed that could offer a 69% increase in allowable design bending strength compared with the currently available strength value in existing standards.

Flatwise Bending Strength (F_{by})

The 5th percentile (at 75% tolerance) flatwise MOR was calculated from the data shown in Figure 17, which resulted in a value of 4,130 lb/in^2. Design values for beams in the flatwise orientation (vertically laminated) were based on a 12-in.-deep member, and our experimental beams were only 3-1/8-in. deep. The flat-use factor from AITC 117 (AITC 1993) that converts from a 3-1/8-in. to a 12-in. depth is 1.16. Using Equation (2), the allowable design bending strength F_{by} was determined to be 1,970 lb/in^2. After applying the flat-use factor, this value was 1,695 lb/in^2. This compares favorably with the homogeneous L3 combination, which has an F_{by} value of 800 lb/in^2, resulting in a 111% improvement over the comparable combination in existing standards.

Shear Strength (F_{vx})

The 5th percentile (at 75% tolerance) shear strength based on a censored data analysis and a lognormal distribution was 156 lb/in^2. Using Equation (2), the allowable design shear strength F_{vx} was determined to be 74 lb/in^2. This value is significantly lower than that published for the all-L3 Western Woods combination of 120 lb/in^2. This leads us to believe that the published design shear strength value for glulam beams made with Western Wood core laminations may be non-conservative when applied to glulam beams with ponderosa pine core laminations.

Tension Strength (F_t)

The 5th percentile (at 75% tolerance) tensile strength was calculated from the data shown in Figure 19, which resulted in a value of 2,140 lb/in^2. Using Equation (2), the allowable design tensile strength F_t was determined to be 1,020 lb/in^2. This compares favorably to two industry standards and results in a 94% improvement over the homogeneous L3 combination, which has an F_t value of 525 lb/in^2. In addition, the ASTM D 3737 standard (ASTM 2000a) does not have any provisions for calculating glulam tension strength, based on the properties of the laminating lumber. So, the relationship in the D 3737 standard assumes that design tensile strength (F_t) is 5/8 times the value of the design edgewise bending strength (F_{bx}). The ratio that we found experimentally was 0.70, with a 95% confidence interval of 0.58 to 0.83. This confidence interval is based on the assumption of lognormal distributions for both the tensile and bending strengths. These results confirm that the ASTM D 3737 5/8 factor is adequate for these beams.

Solid-Sawn Lumber Properties

To gauge the relative quality of the lumber used in this study, we compared the mechanical properties of our core lamination grade to past data on No. 2 grade ponderosa pine lumber. The average MOE of our core lamination grade (1.11×10^6 lb/in^2) exceeded the value from the In-Grade Testing Program (0.98×10^6 lb/in^2, Green and Evans 1987) and by far exceeded the value observed in the Emmett, Idaho, study (0.86×10^6 lb/in^2), which was also derived from a small-diameter timber resource (Table 3; Gorman and Green 2000). For edgewise bending strength, our core lamination grade achieved an average MOR value of 4,600 lb/in^2 (Table 9), which was lower than the In-Grade average MOR for No. 2 grade ponderosa pine (5,290 lb/in^2), yet was higher than the Emmett data (3,880 lb/in^2). For shear strength, the core lamination grade had an average shear strength of 875 lb/in^2, which exceeded the ASTM D 2555 value of 795 lb/in^2 (adjusted to 12% moisture content). Overall, we observed that although this set of lumber had higher stiffness and shear strength properties, it was lower in bending strength properties than the ponderosa pine lumber tested in the In-Grade Testing Program (Green and Evans 1987). This indicates that lumber processed from small-diameter timber resources is more likely to have a higher percentage of juvenile wood and thus has lower strength properties in tension and bending.

Comparison of Experimental and Alllowable Properties

In summary, Table 12 compares allowable glulam beam properties determined experimentally in this study and allowable properties for the all-L3 homogeneous beam combination currently available in the glulam standards. The ratio for our results (Fig. 2) and the all-L3 combination was also determined.

ASTM D 3737 Re-Analysis

A final analysis of the glulam beam combination involved re-analysis of the bending strength and stiffness values using actual measured lumber properties. In place of the assumed lumber properties in Table 4, we used the actual lumber

MOE values for the three zones of lumber grades and the actual knot properties for the 1.4E grades reported in Table 7. The knot properties used for the No. 2 grade of lumber were the same as those reported in Table 4.

The re-analysis of the 8-lamination beam indicated a design glulam MOE of 1.190×10^6 lb/in^2 and a design bending strength (F_{bx}) of 1,279 lb/in^2. The re-analysis of the 13-lamination beam indicated a design glulam MOE of 1.234×10^6 lb/in^2 and a design bending strength of 1,328 lb/in^2. The design glulam MOE value was again calculated to be 1.2×10^6 lb/in^2 using ASTM D 3737 procedures, and the fact that the experimental results exceeded this level shows that this target MOE level is technically feasible. The design bending strength, on the other hand, was calculated to be approximately 1,300 lb/in^2 using the D 3737 procedures. This level, however, is based on the use of a special tension lamination. Because we did not use a special tension lamination grade, D 3737 procedures require that this design bending stress be reduced to 1,100 lb/in^2 for beams ≤15 in. deep and 975 lb/in^2 for beams >15 in. deep. Because our experimental results showed that this beam combination can achieve a design bending strength of approximately 1,400 lb/in^2, this leads us to believe that the special tension lamination requirements calculated by the D 3737 standard are not accurate for design stresses as low as these. In other words, special tension lamination grades were developed to ensure that glulam beams having higher design bending stress values, in the range of 2,200 to 2,400 lb/in^2, achieve these levels of strength. Without considering this special tension lamination adjustment, the difference between the experimentally determined design bending strength and the calculated design bending strength was approximately 10%.

In addition, the ANSI/AITC A190.1 standard requires that the 5th percentile finger-joint tensile strength value must achieve a level of strength that is 1.67 times the design bending strength of glulam beams. This ratio of finger-joint 5th percentile to glulam design bending strength is referred to as the qualification stress level (QSL). We calculated a QSL factor from our test data of 1.17 (1,690 lb/in^2/1,440 lb/in^2), which is well below the required 1.67 factor. When calculating a similar qualification stress level based on the 5th percentile solid-sawn lumber tensile strength of the 1.4-1/4 grade from Table 9, we found the ratio to be 1.52 (2,195/1,440 lb/in^2).

Conclusions

This study involved the evaluation of ponderosa pine glulam made from lumber sawn from a small-diameter timber resource. Lumber sawn from small-diameter ponderosa pine was found to be feasible for the development of E-rated lumber grades, having average MOE values of 1.0 and 1.4×10^6 lb/in^2. We observed that approximately 66% of this lumber resource would qualify for these E-rated lumber grades.

Table 12—Comparison of allowable design values for ponderosa pine glulam

Property	Allowable design value		
	Calculated in study	All-L3 grade combination	Ratio of study to L3 combination
F_{bx} (lb/in^2)	1,440	850	1.69
F_{by} (lb/in^2)	1,695	800	2.12
F_t (lb/in^2)	1,020	500	2.04
F_{vx} (lb/in^2)	74	120	0.62
MOE (10^6 lb/in^2)	1.34	1.00	1.34

Two different glulam beam depths were evaluated: 8 and 13 laminations. The 8-lamination glulam beam combination was targeted for F_{bx} and F_t tests and the 13-lamination glulam beam combination for F_{bx}, F_{by}, and F_{vx} tests. Beam deflection was measured during these strength tests, and a variety of glulam MOE values were determined. The calculated design values for the various mechanical properties of this new ponderosa pine glulam beam combination were compared to the published design values of the L3 glulam combination (combination 22 from AITC 117). Overall, we determined that using mechanically graded lumber in the glulam combination resulted in a structural member that efficiently utilized this small-diameter ponderosa pine resource. The calculated design values of this new glulam combination are a significant improvement over the published design values of the all ponderosa pine L3-grade combination that is currently available in the standards.

Analysis of the glulam beam and laminating lumber test results showed that the industry standard volume effect exponent of 0.10 is appropriate for these ponderosa pine glulam beams. The ratio of glulam tensile strength (F_t) to glulam bending strength (F_{bx}) was found to be 0.70, which further supports the industry standard value of 5/8 (0.625). Finally, the qualification stress levels of finger-jointed and solid-sawn lumber tensile strength were found to be 1.17 and 1.52 times that of the calculated design bending strength of the glulam beams. These two values are significantly lower than the industry standard value of 1.67, which indicates that there may be a grade-dependent or layup effect on this qualification stress level factor.

Literature Cited

AITC. 2004. Standard specifications for structural glued laminated timber of softwood species. AITC 117–04. Englewood, CO: American Institute of Timber Construction. http://www.aitc-glulam.org/

ASTM. 2000a. Standard practice for establishing stresses for structural glued laminated timber (glulam). Vol. 4.10, ASTM D 3737–99. West Conshohocken, PA: American Society for Testing and Materials. http://www.astm.org/

ASTM. 2000b. Standard test methods for static tests of lumber in structural sizes. Vol. 4.10, ASTM D 198–99. American Society for Testing and Materials, West Conshohocken, PA. http://www.astm.org/

ASTM. 2000c. Standard practice for establishing structural grades and related allowable properties for visually graded lumber. Vol. 4.10, ASTM D245–99. West Conshohocken, PA: American Society for Testing and Materials. http://www.astm.org/

Burns, R.M.; Honkala, B.H. 1990. Silvics of North America. Vol. I, Conifers. Agric. Handb. 654. Washington, DC: U.S. Department of Agriculture, Forest Service. 675 p.

Erickson, R.G.; Gorman, T.M.; Green, D.W.; Graham, D. 2000. Mechanical grading of lumber sawn from small-diameter lodgepole pine, ponderosa pine, and grand fir trees from northern Idaho. Forest Products Journal. 50(7/8):59–65.

Forest Products Laboratory. 2000. Forest Products Laboratory research program on small-diameter material. Gen. Tech. Rep. FPL–GTR–110 (Rev.). Madison, WI: U.S. Department of Agriculture, Forest Service, Forest Products Laboratory. 31 p.

Gorman, T.M.; Green, D.W. 2000. Mechanical grading of lumber sawn from small-diameter Rocky Mountain species. In: Proc., Gazo, R., ed. Issues related to handling the influx of small-diameter timber in western North America. No. 7261, Madison, WI. Forest Products Society: 29–35.

Green, D.W.; Evans, J.W. 1987. Mechanical properties of visually graded dimension lumber. NTIS PB–88–159–371, vol. 1–7. Springfield, VA: National Technical Information Service.

Hernandez, R.; Moody, R.C.; Falk, R.H. 1995. Fiber stress values for design of glulam timber utility structures. FPL–RP–532. Madison, WI: U.S. Department of Agriculture, Forest Service, Forest Products Laboratory. 23 p.

Lowell, E.C.; Green, D.W. 2000. Lumber recovery from small-diameter ponderosa pine from Flagstaff, AZ. In: Proc. RMRS–P–22. Fort Collins, CO: U.S. Department of Agriculture, Forest Service, Rocky Mountain Research Station.

NDS. 1997. National design specification for wood construction. Supplement. Washington, DC: American Forest & Paper Association, American Wood Council. http://www.awc.org/

Simpson, W.T.; Green, D.W. 2001. Effect of drying methods on warp and grade of 2 by 4's from small-diameter ponderosa pine. Res. Pap. FPL–RP–601. Madison, WI: U.S. Department of Agriculture, Forest Service, Forest Products Laboratory. 17 p.

Voorhies, G.; Gorman, W.A. 1982. Longitudinal shrinkage and occurrence of various fibril angles in juvenile wood of young-growth ponderosa pine. Arizona Forestry Notes 16. Flagstaff, AZ: University of Northern Arizona.

WWPA. 2000. Western lumber grading rules. Portland, OR: Western Wood Products Association.

Yeh, B. 1997. Shear strength of structural glued laminated timber based on full size flexure tests. APA Rep. T97–25. Tacoma, WA: APA–The Engineered Wood Association.

Appendix A—Glulam Beam Maps of Lumber MOE Values

The following figures are glulam beam maps for the 8- and 13-lamination beams tested in this study. The MOE values were determined using the continuous lumber tester (CLT) at the laminating plant and were not adjusted. The location of finger joints, accurate to within 1/4-ft, is indicated on each map.

8-Lamination Beam Maps (Edgewise Specimens)

Beam 08-01

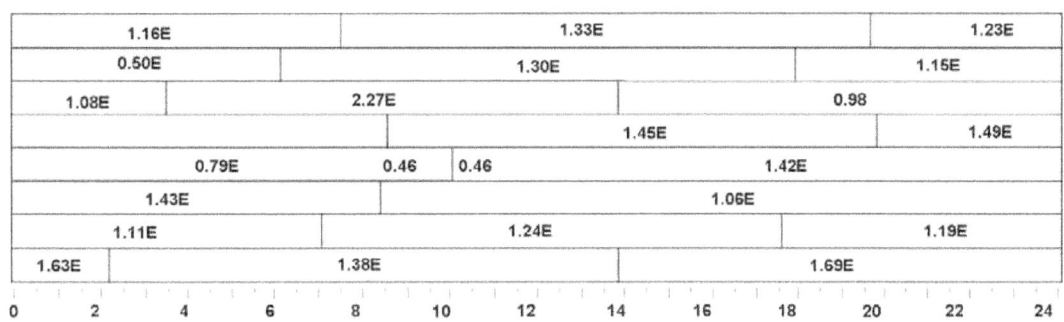

Beam 08-02

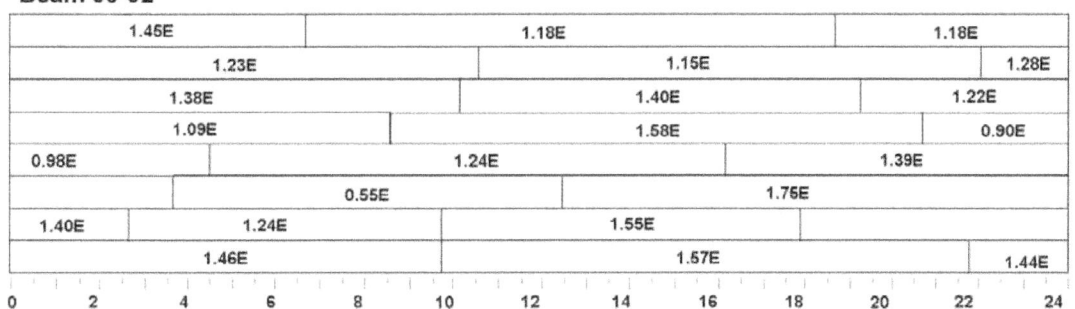

Beam 08-03

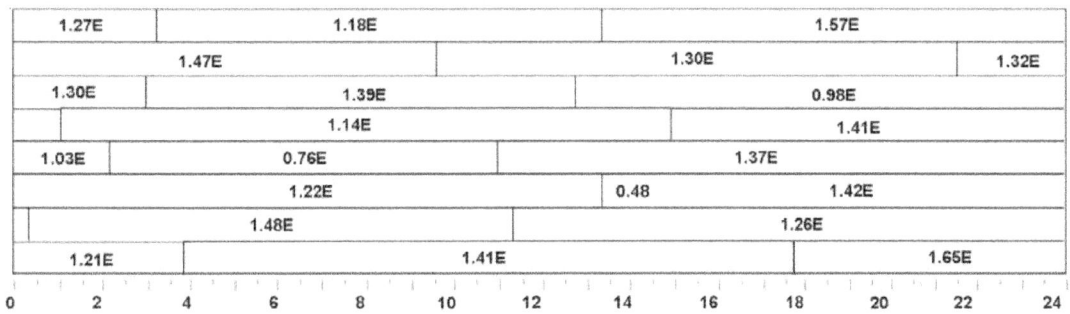

Beam 08-04

1.15E	1.32E	
1.12E	1.19E	
1.09E	1.40E	
1.20E	1.50E	
1.91E	0.97E	
1.35E	1.26E	1.57E
1.31E	0.88E	1.25E · 1.37E
1.39E	1.21E	1.23E

0 2 4 6 8 10 12 14 16 18 20 22 24

Beam 08-05

1.44E	1.31E		
1.19E			
1.31E	0.98E	0.98E	
1.58E	1.89E	1.19E	0.94E
1.26E	1.22E	1.48E	1.24E
1.22E	1.22E		

0 2 4 6 8 10 12 14 16 18 20 22 24

Beam 08-06

1.28E	1.33E	0.72E	
1.15E	1.11E		
1.13E	1.31E	1.24E	
1.22E	0.87E	0.99E	
1.55E	1.41E	0.44E	0.79E
0.90E	1.24E		
1.38E	1.25E		
1.34E	1.57E	1.38E	

0 2 4 6 8 10 12 14 16 18 20 22 24

Beam 08-07

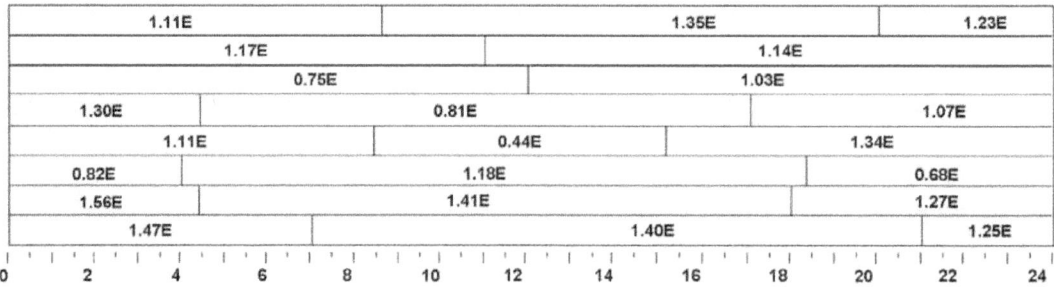

1.11E	1.35E	1.23E
1.17E	1.14E	
0.75E	1.03E	
1.30E	0.81E	1.07E
1.11E	0.44E	1.34E
0.82E	1.18E	0.68E
1.56E	1.41E	1.27E
1.47E	1.40E	1.25E

0 2 4 6 8 10 12 14 16 18 20 22 24

20

Beam 08-08

1.14E		1.21E
1.12E		1.27E
0.86E	1.22E	1.17E
0.67E	1.03E	1.20E
1.21E	1.11E	0.93E
0.87E	1.30E	0.67E	0.84E
1.35E	1.38E	1.34E
1.46E	1.26E	1.22E

0   2   4   6   8   10   12   14   16   18   20   22   24

Beam 08-09

1.16E		1.11E
1.13E	1.46E	1.20E
1.22E	1.24E	0.62E
0.65E	1.17E	0.94E
1.11E	0.68E	1.07E
0.82E	1.20E	0.59E
1.23E	1.34E
1.66E	1.42E

0   2   4   6   8   10   12   14   16   18   20   22   24

Beam 08-10

1.21E		1.63E
1.65E	1.21E	1.13E
1.07E	0.80E
1.62E	1.10E
1.15E	1.20E	0.81E
1.09E	0.87E	0.59E
1.36E	1.21E	1.35E
1.54E	1.34E	1.12E

0   2   4   6   8   10   12   14   16   18   20   22   24

Beam 08-11

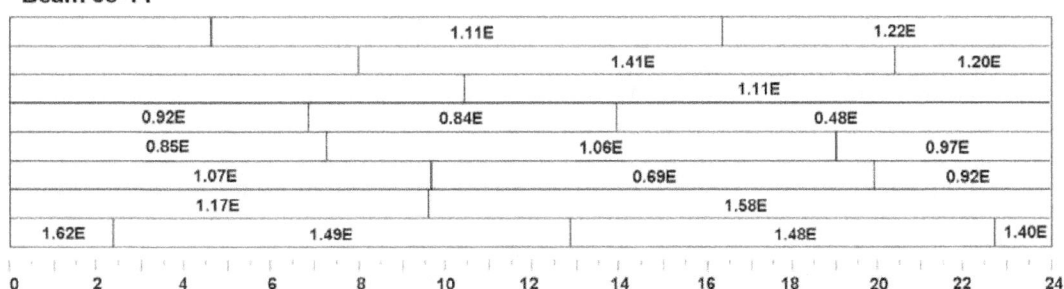

1.11E		1.22E
1.41E		1.20E
1.11E		
0.92E	0.84E	0.48E
0.85E	1.06E	0.97E
1.07E	0.69E	0.92E
1.17E	1.58E
1.62E	1.49E	1.48E	1.40E

0   2   4   6   8   10   12   14   16   18   20   22   24

Beam 08-12

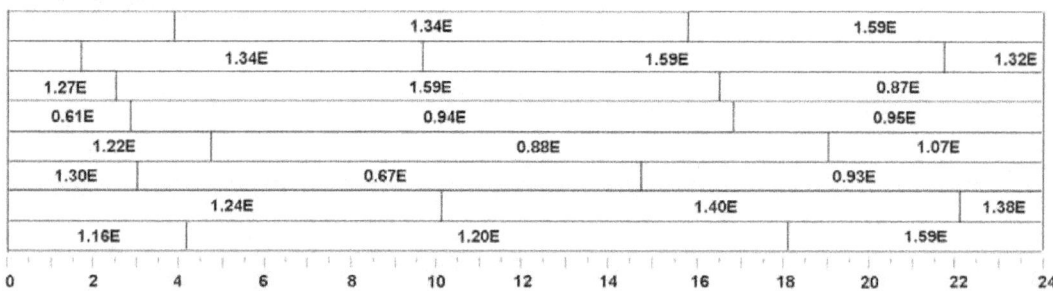

Beam 08-13

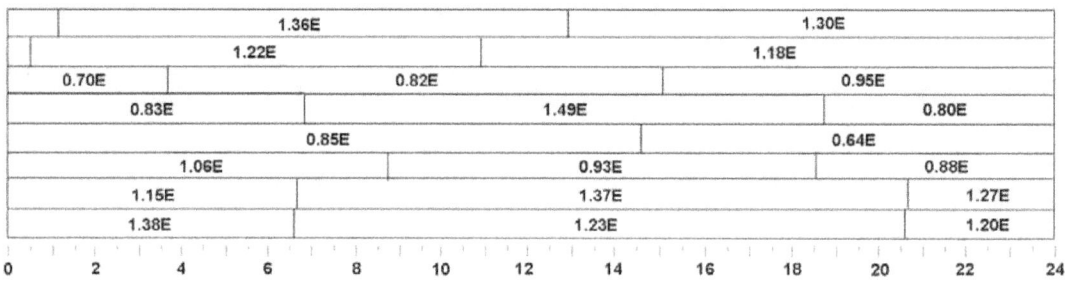

Beam 08-14

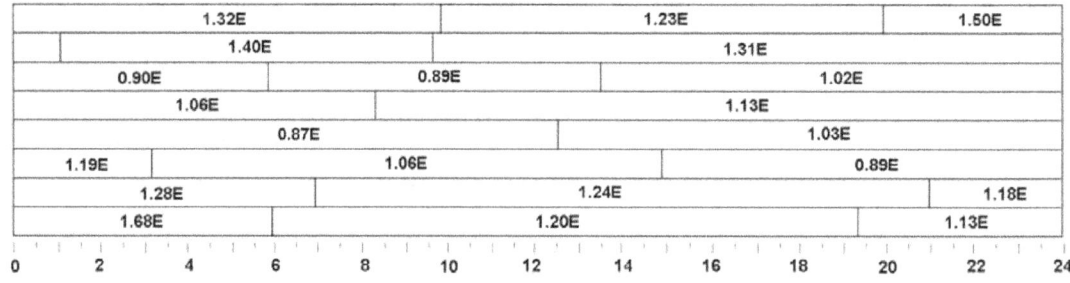

Beam 08-15

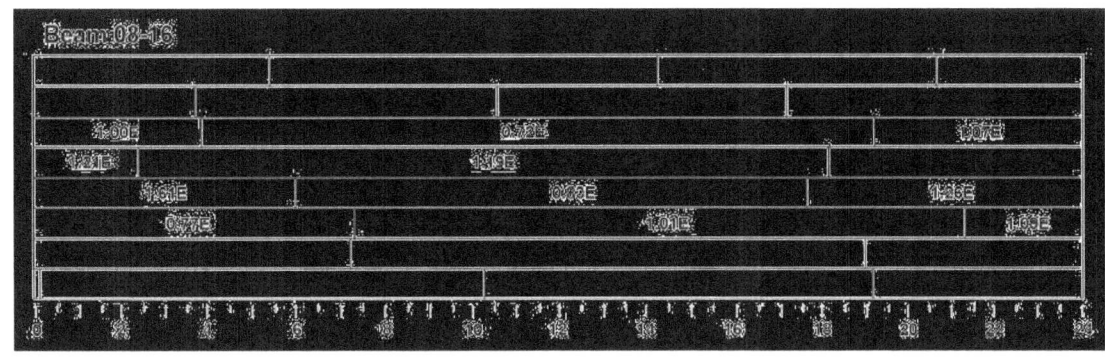

13-Lamination Beam Maps (Edgewise, Flatwise, and Shear Specimens)

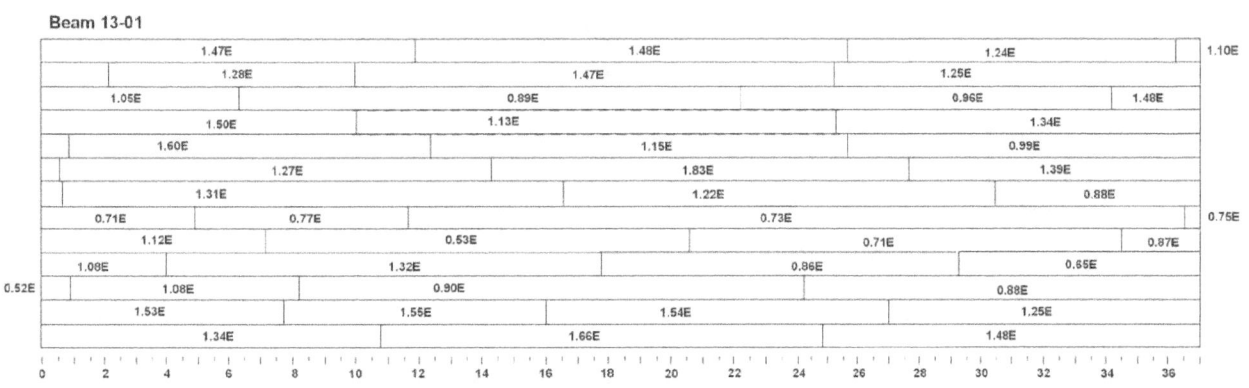

Beam 13-01

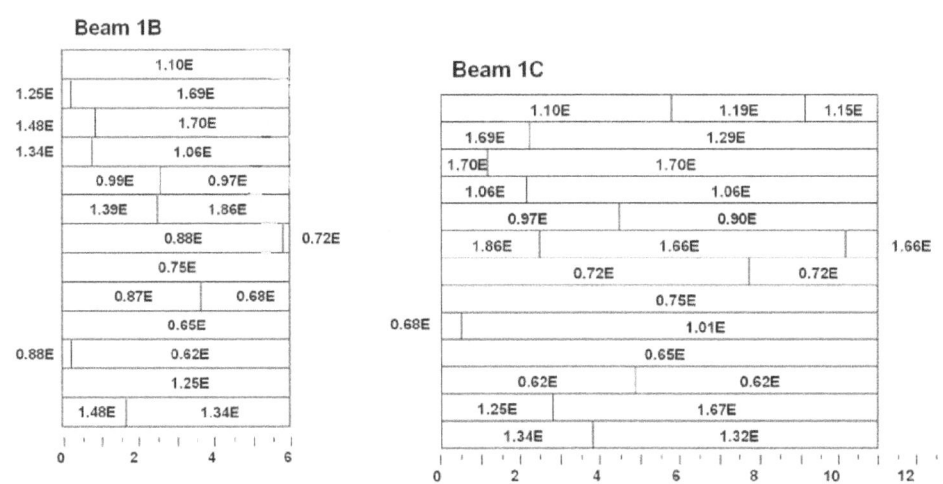

Beam 1B

Beam 1C

Beam 13-02

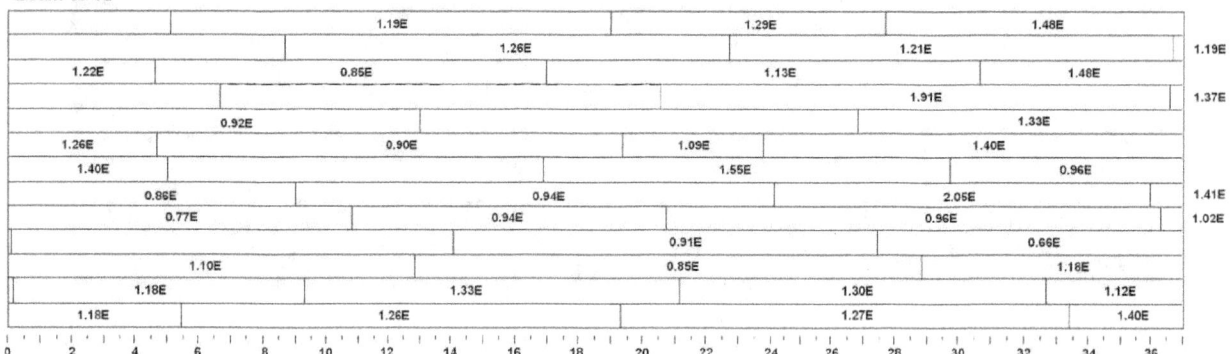

Beam 2B

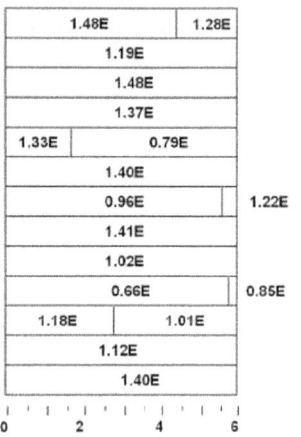

Beam 2C

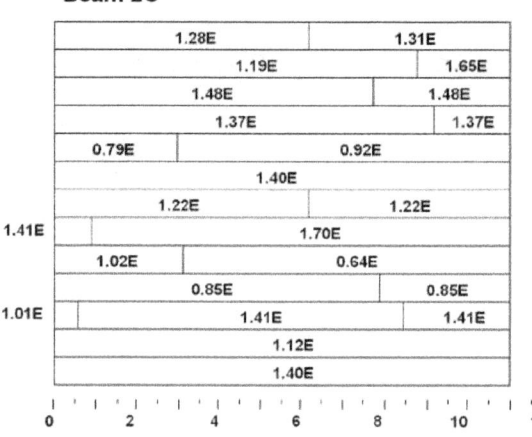

Beam 13-03

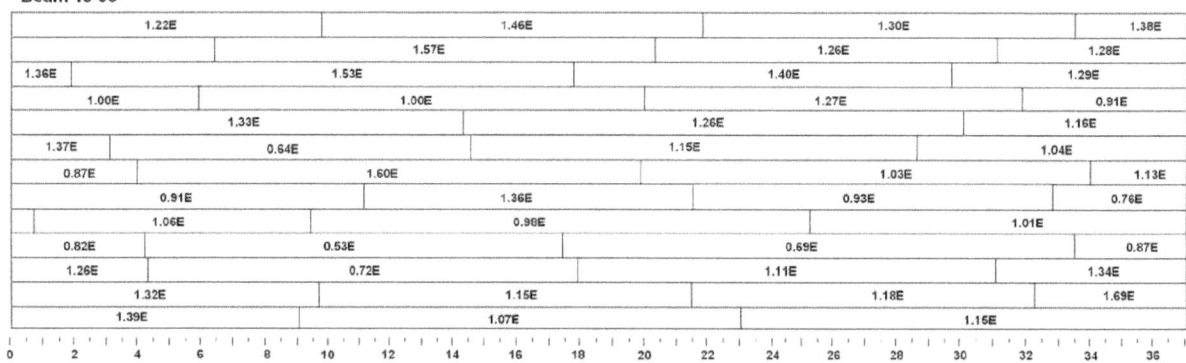

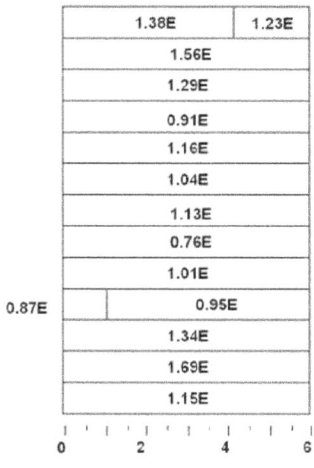

Beam 3B

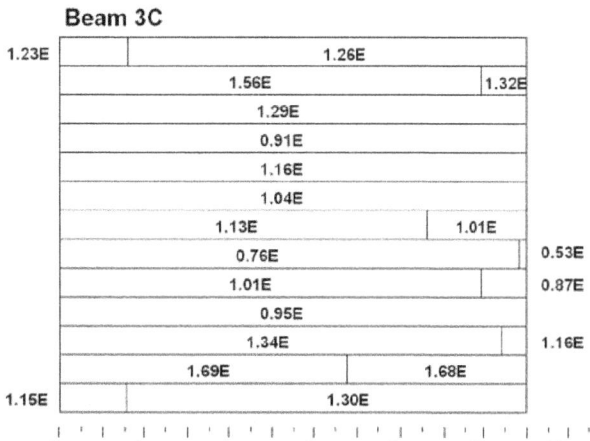

Beam 3C

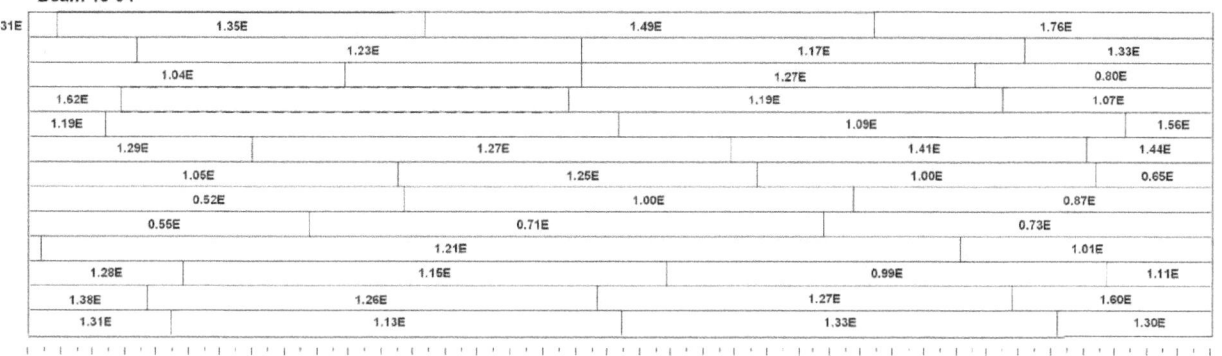

Beam 13-04

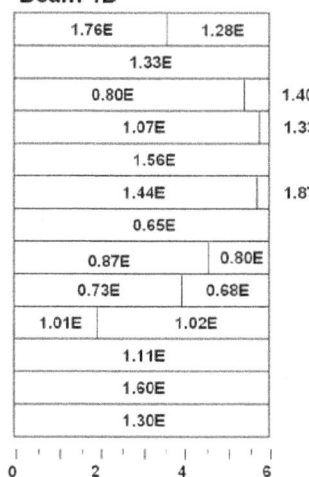

Beam 4B

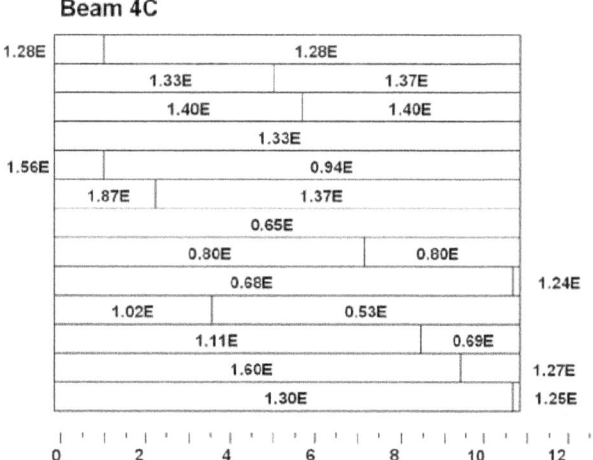

Beam 4C

25

Beam 13-05

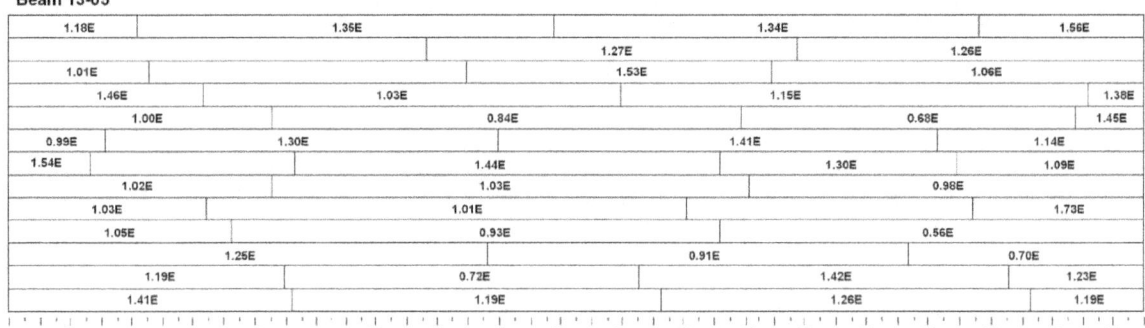

Beam 5B

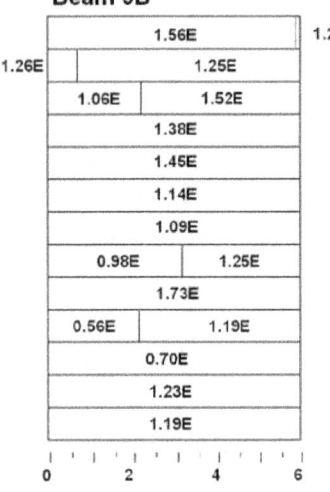

Beam 5C

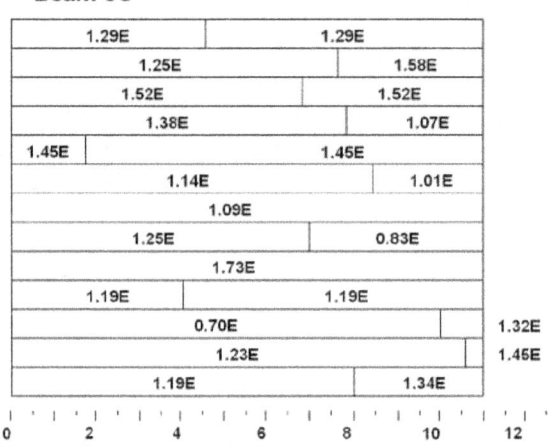

Beam 13-06

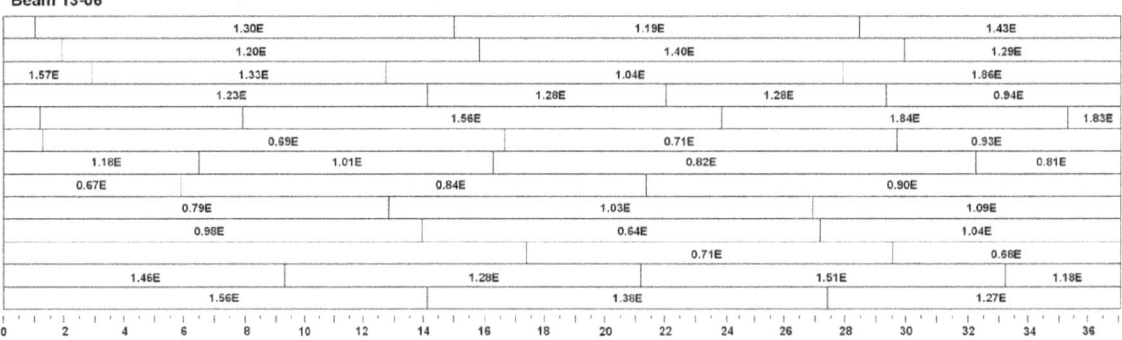

Beam 6B

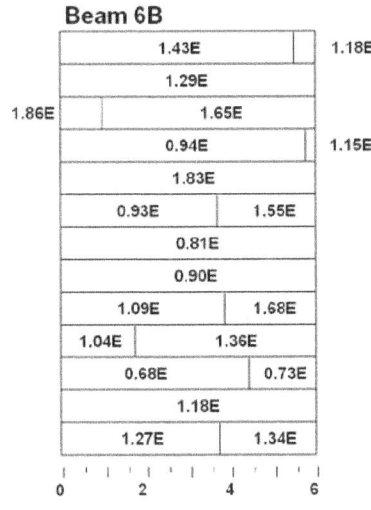

Beam 6C

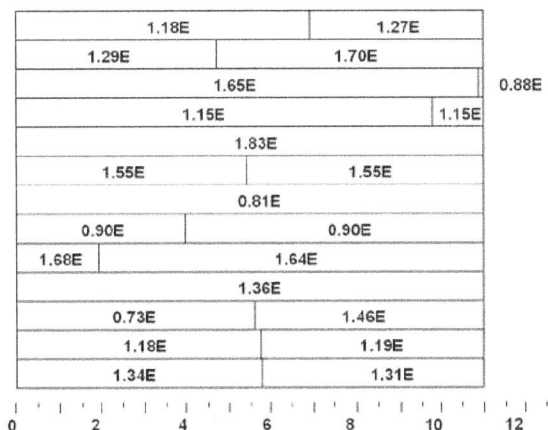

Beam 13-07

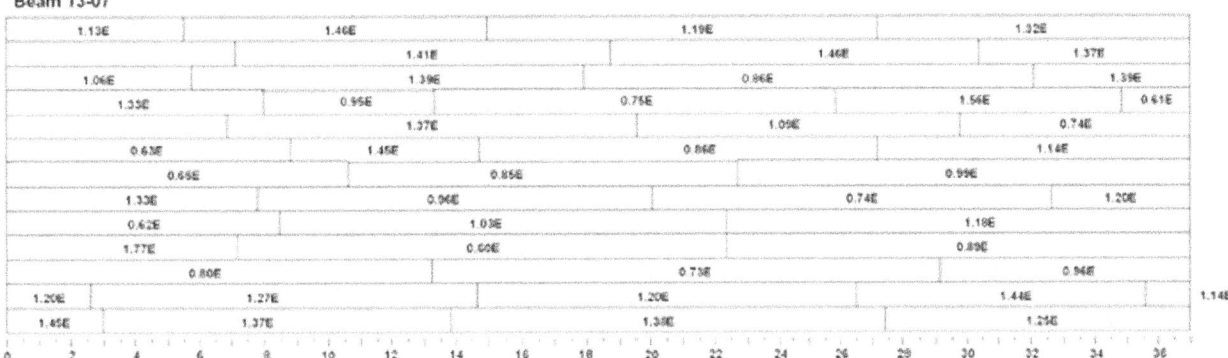

Beam 7B

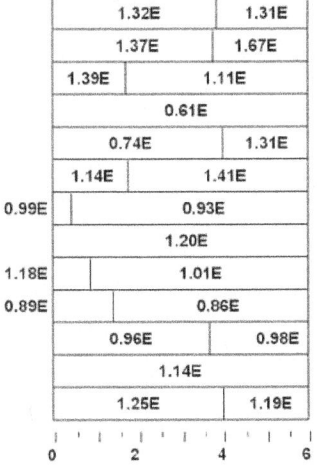

Beam 7C

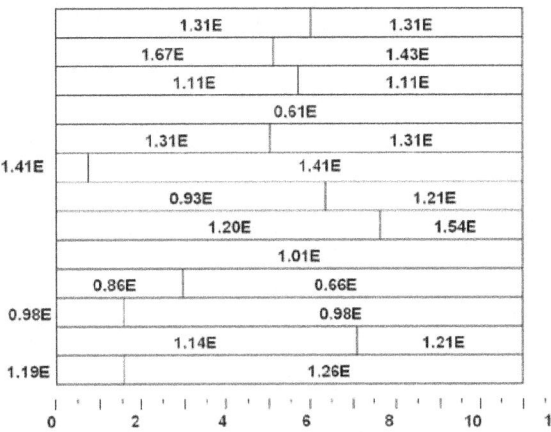

Beam 13-08

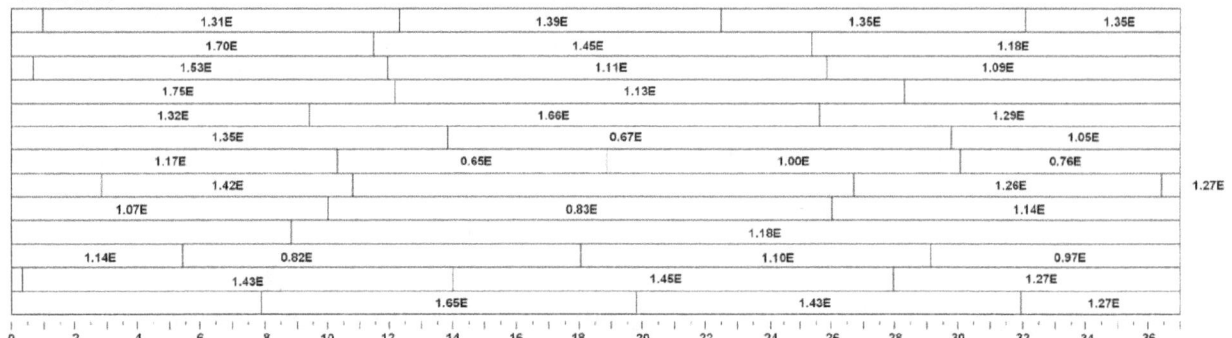

Beam 8B

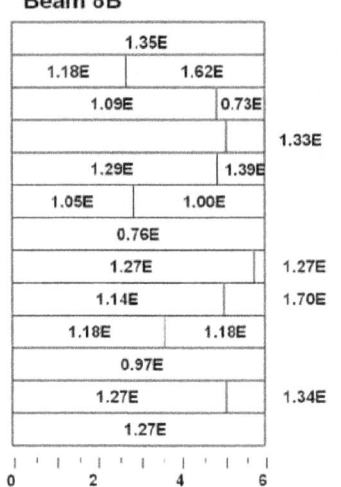

Beam 8C

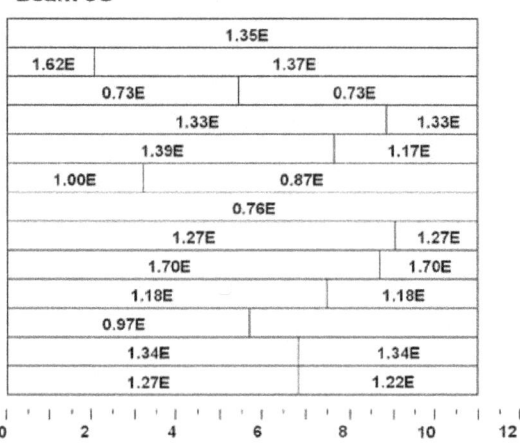

Beam 13-09

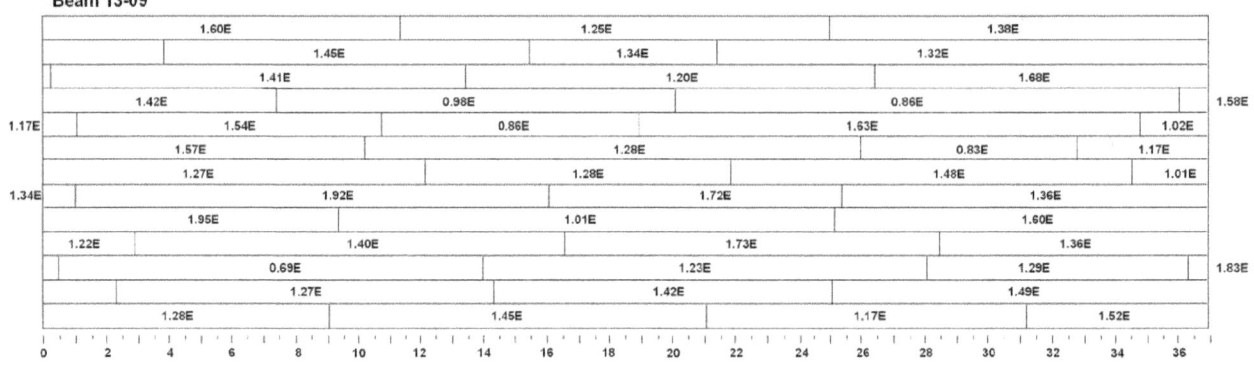

Beam 9B

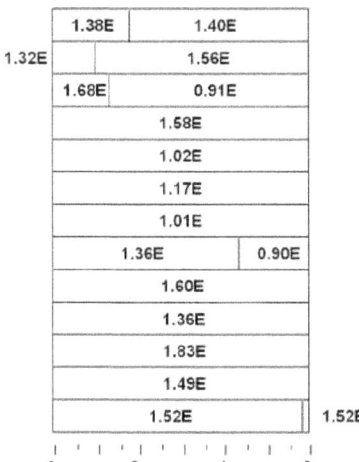

Beam 9C

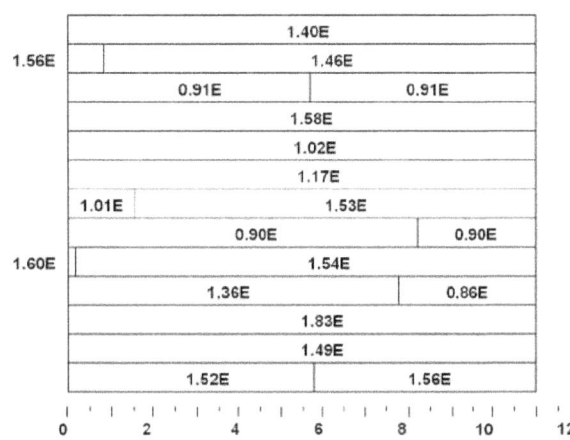

Beam 13-10

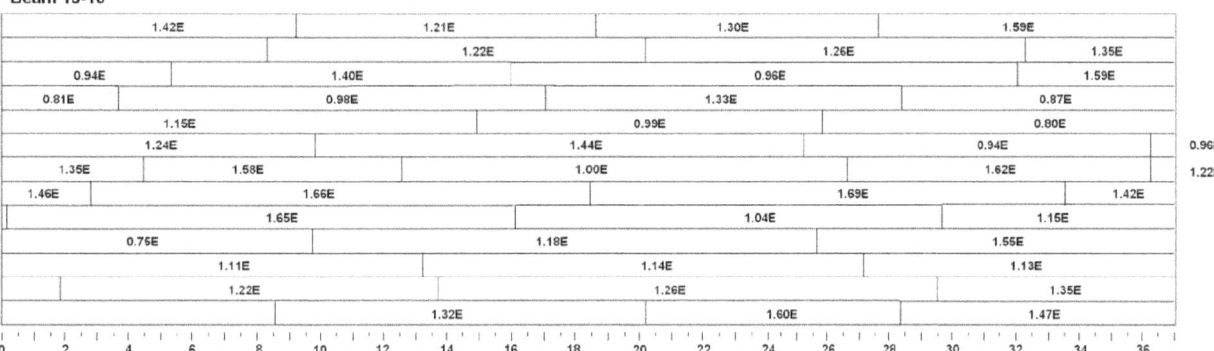

Beam 10B

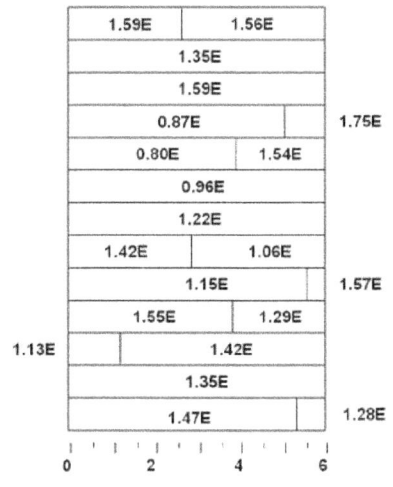

Beam 10C

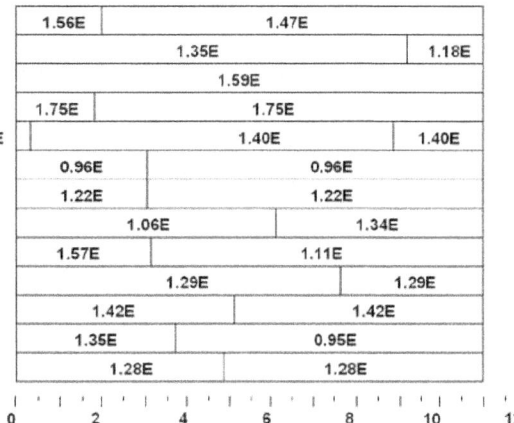

Beam 13-11

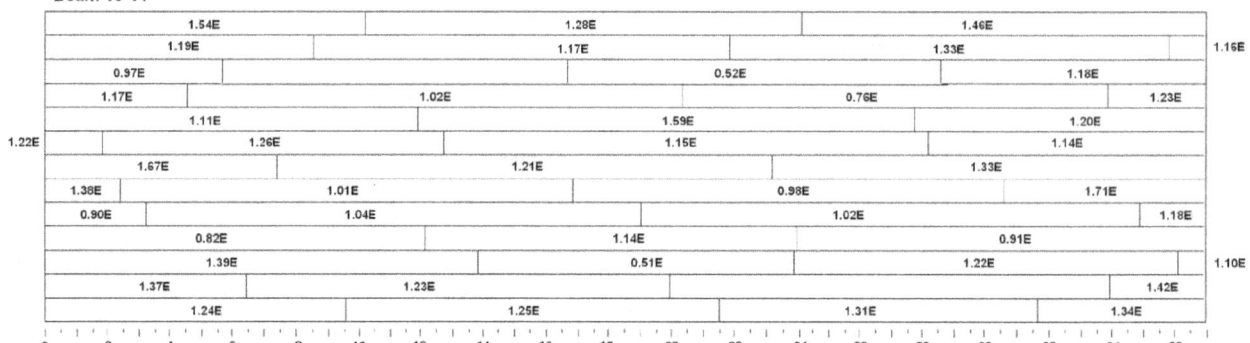

Beam 11B

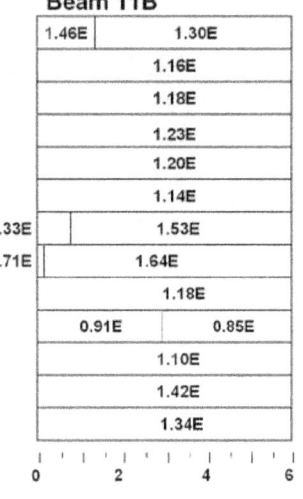

Beam 11C

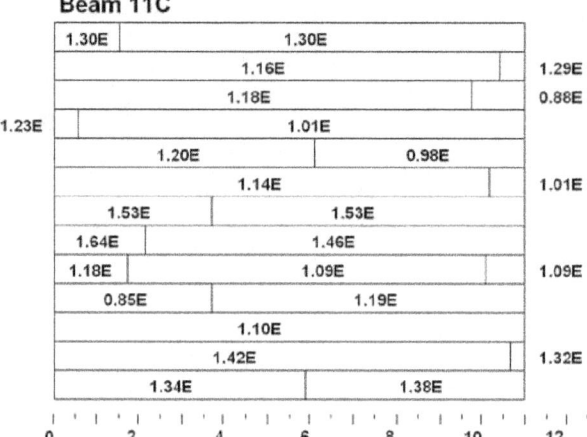

Beam 13-12

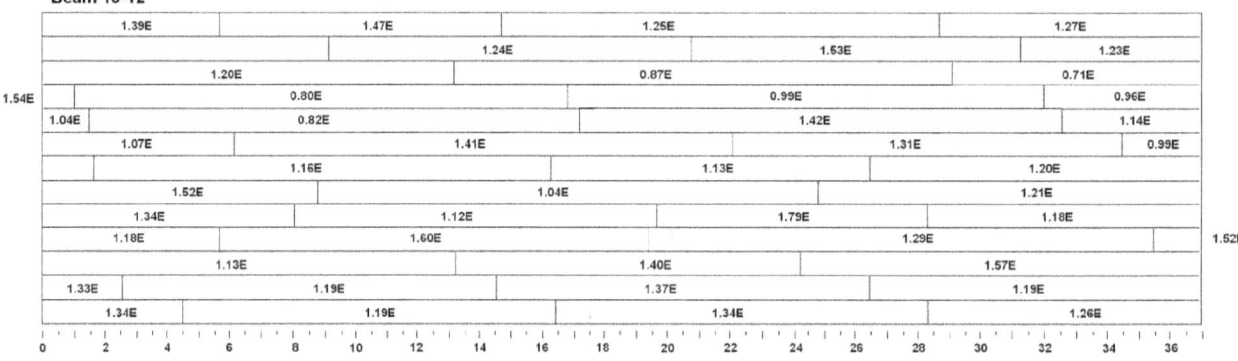

Beam 12B

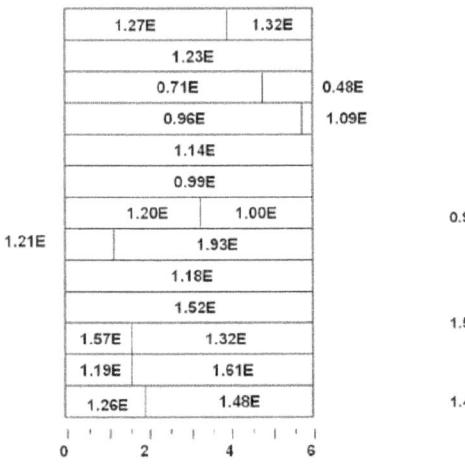

Beam 12C

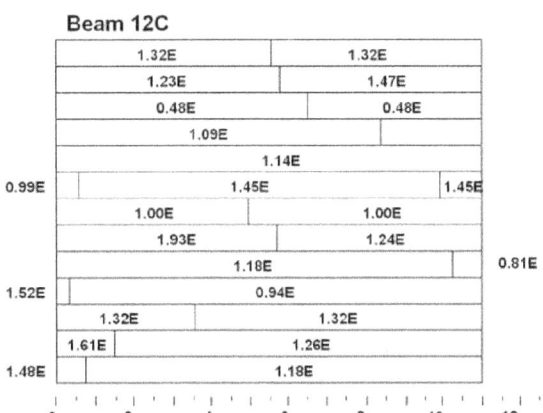

Beam 13-13

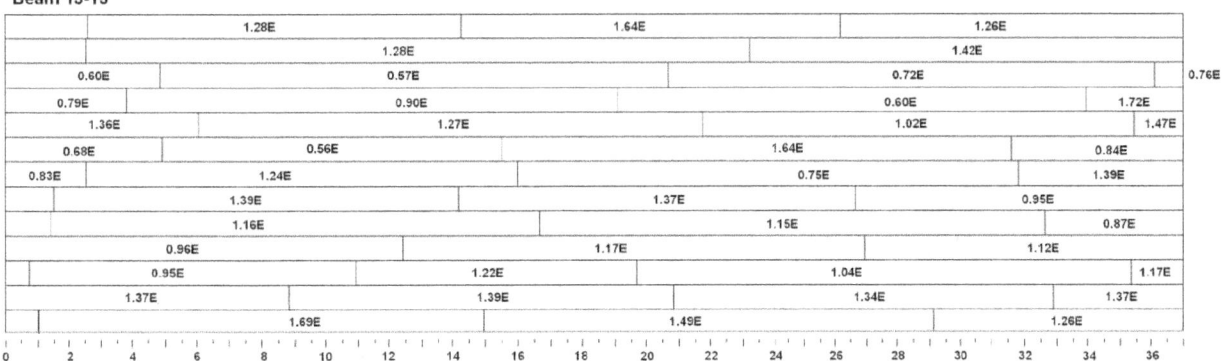

Beam 13B

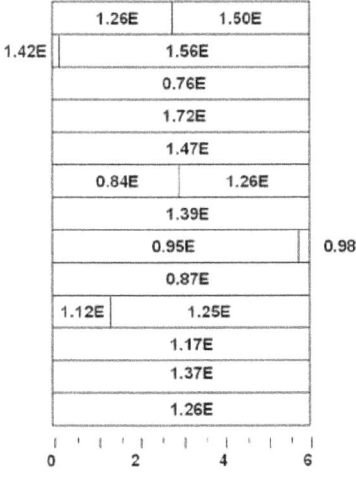

Beam 13C

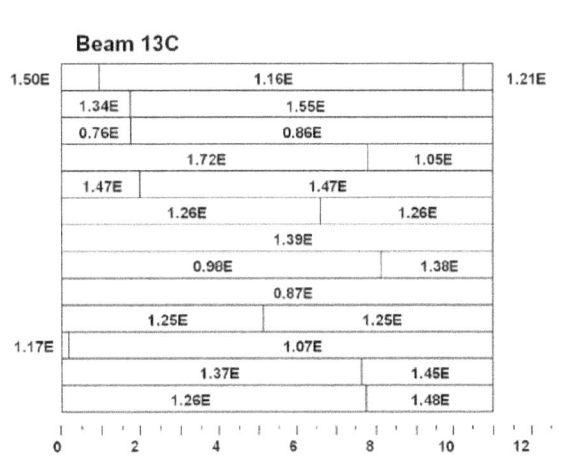

Beam 13-14

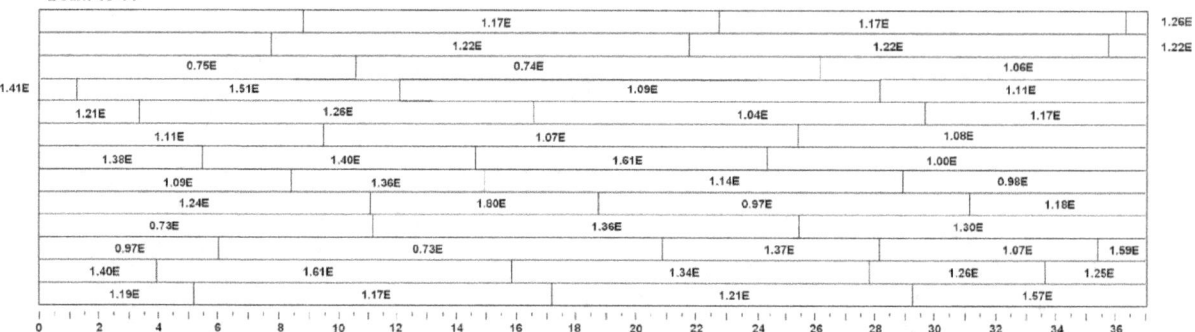

Beam 14B

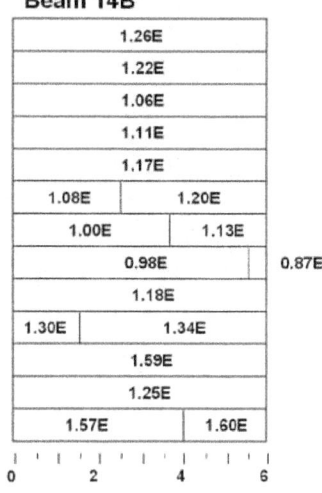

Beam 14C

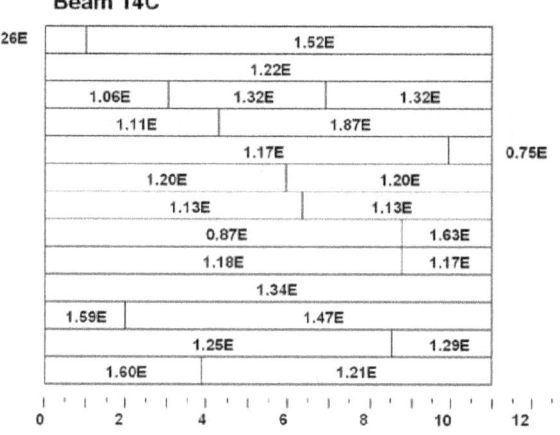

Beam 13-15

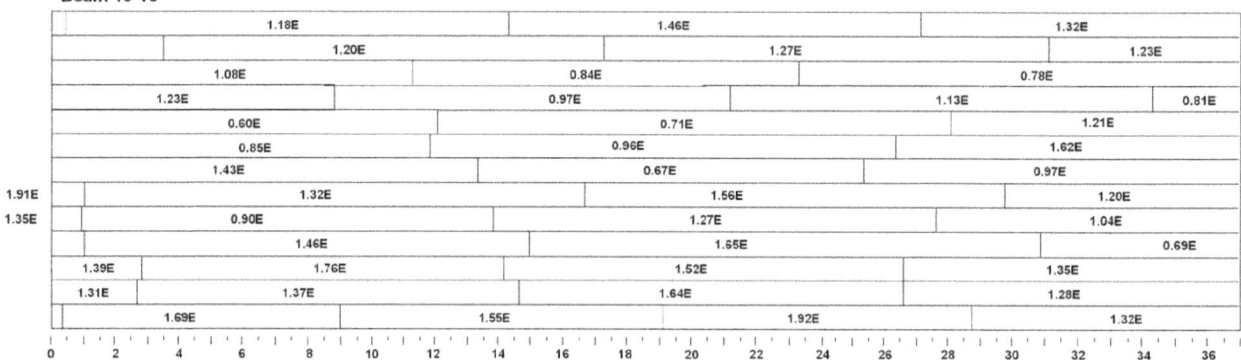

32

Beam 15B

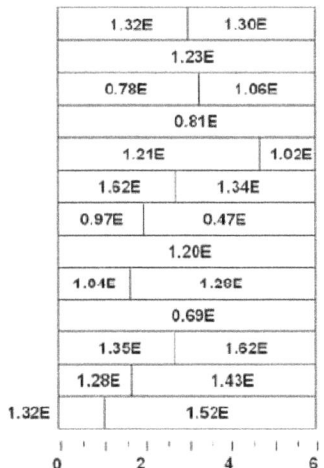

Beam 15C

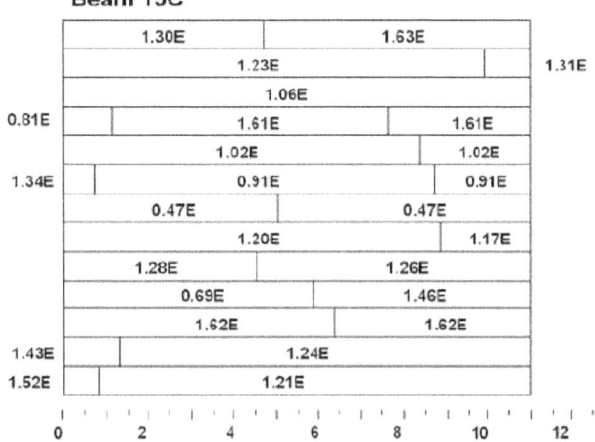

Beam 13-16

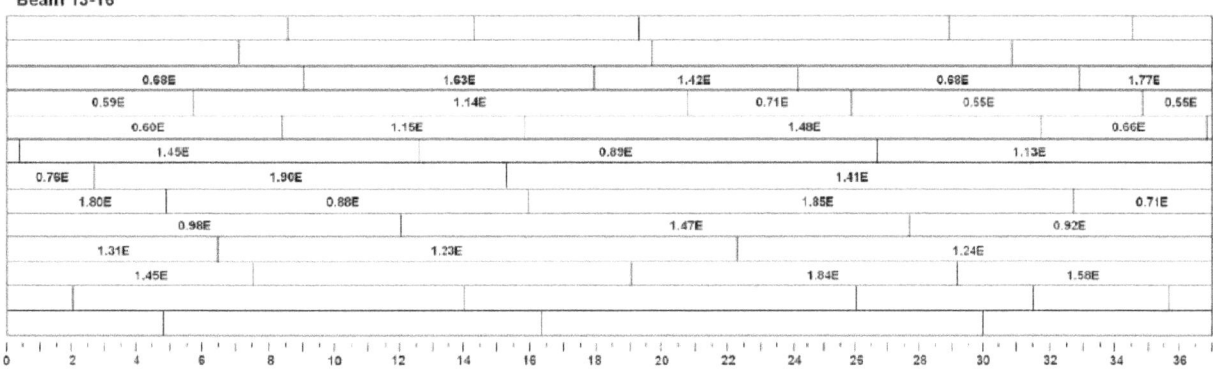

Beam 16B

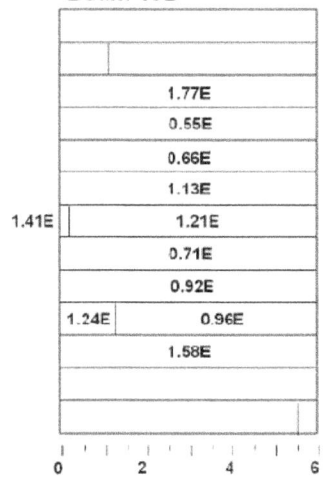

Beam 16C

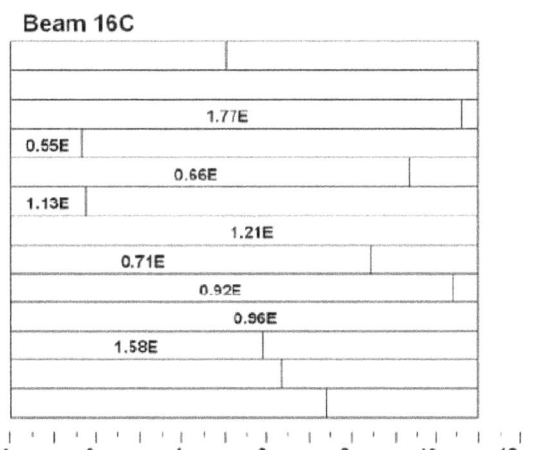

Appendix B—Knot Properties of Ponderosa Pine Laminating Lumber

The ASTM D 3737 standard (ASTM 2000a) specifies that at least 1,000 lineal ft of lumber for each grade should be targeted for knot property measurements when a new species or grade of lumber is being established. In this study, we measured the knot properties of the following E-rated grades: 1.4E–1/4, 1.4E–1/2, 1.0E–1/4, and 1.0E–1/2. These grades include the two grades used in the targeted glulam beam combinations as well as two lower-MOE grades that are candidates for future combinations of ponderosa pine glulam. In analyzing these properties, we also conducted a study to evaluate the 1,000 lineal ft requirement on knot property measurements.

Figure B1 shows the calculated x-bar and h values for both individual groups of 60 lineal ft and a cumulative total for the 1.0E–1/2 edge-knot grade. Results vary greatly when measured in only 60 lineal ft increments. However, note that after approximately 500 lineal ft, the cumulative x-bar and h values appear to settle into a constant value. To study this further, Figure B2 was plotted to show the standard error of the estimates from the regression analysis used to calculate the x-bar and h values from Figure B1. Figure B2 shows that the standard error values settle into a constant value after approximately 500 lineal ft.

Because the results with the 1.0E–1/2EK grade indicated that 500 lineal ft was an adequate amount of lumber for measuring knot properties, we targeted measurements for every 500 lineal ft for each remaining E-rated grade of ponderosa pine.

The following figures show calculated x-bar and h values and standard errors of estimates for various ponderosa pine edge-knot grades. For each figure, analysis was conducted on groups of 60 lineal ft and the cumulative total.

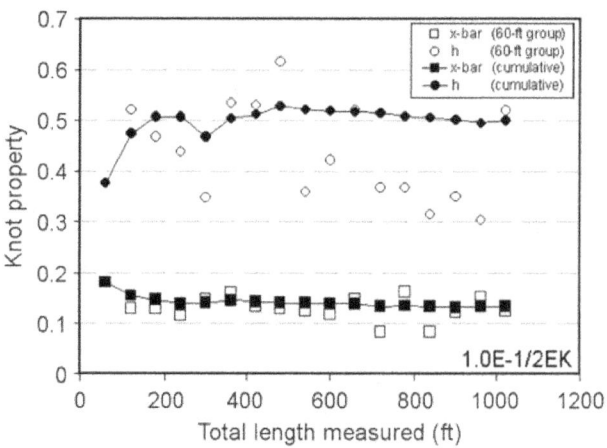

Figure B1—Calculated x-bar and h values for ponderosa pine 1.0E–1/2 EK grade.

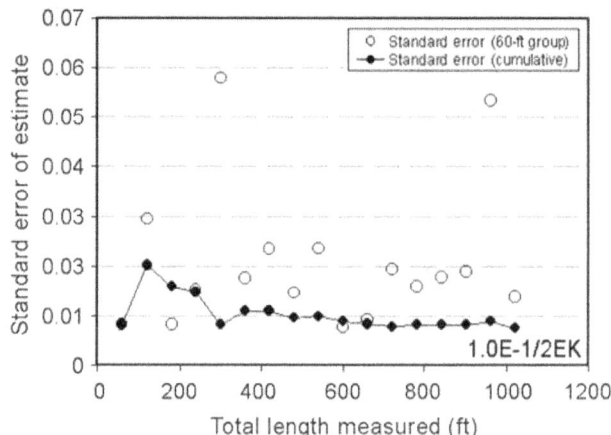

Figure B2—Standard error of estimates from x-bar and h calculations for ponderosa pine 1.0E–1/2 EK grade.

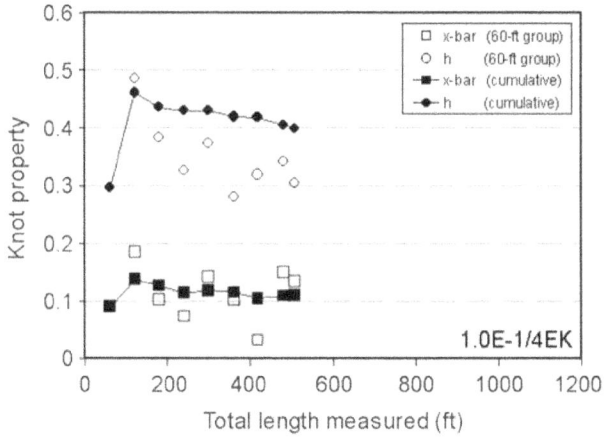

Figure B3—Calculated *x*-bar and *h* values for ponderosa pine 1.0E−1/4 EK grade.

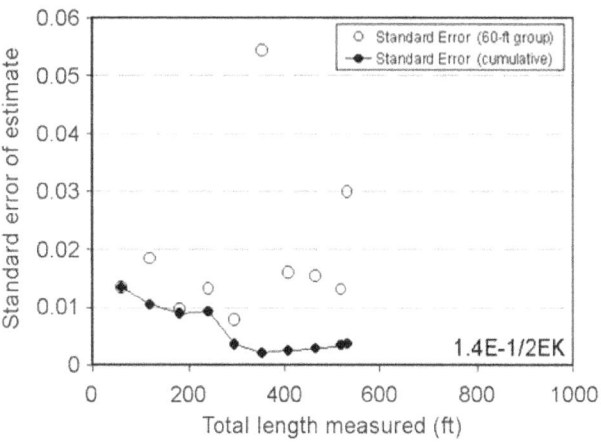

Figure B6—Standard error of estimates from *x*-bar and *h* calculations for ponderosa pine 1.4E−1/2 EK grade.

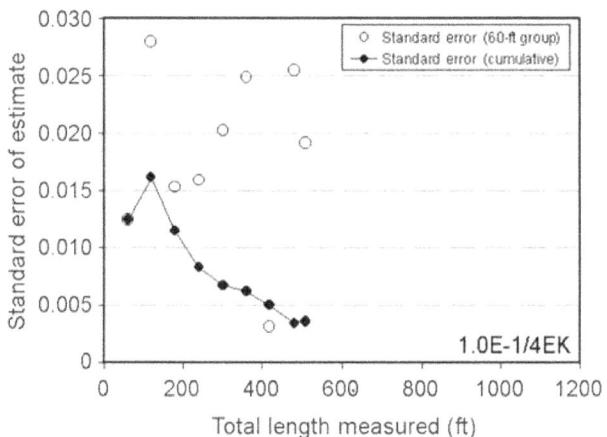

Figure B4—Standard error of estimates from *x*-bar and *h* calculations for ponderosa pine 1.0E−1/4 EK grade.

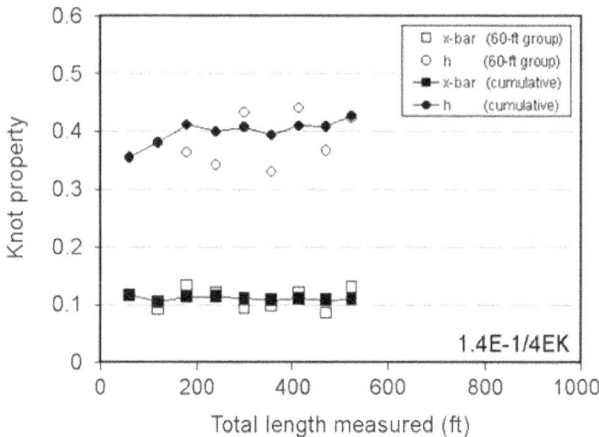

Figure B7—Calculated *x*-bar and *h* values for ponderosa pine 1.4E−1/4 EK grade.

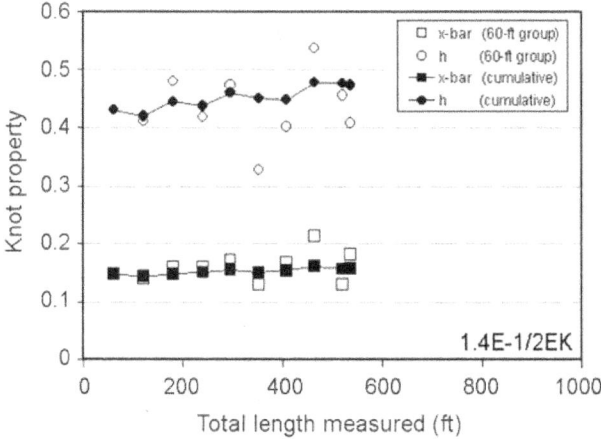

Figure B5—Calculated *x*-bar and *h* values for ponderosa pine 1.4E−1/2 EK grade.

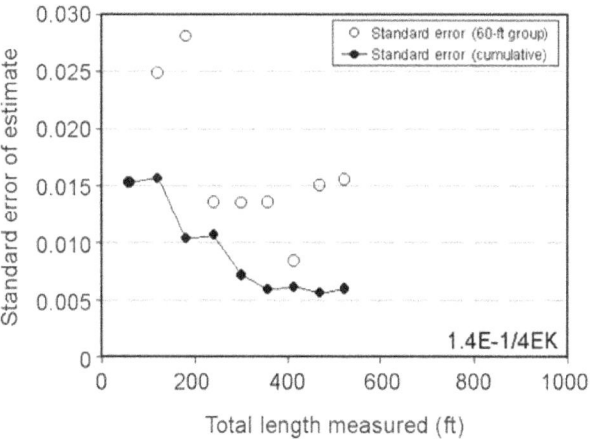

Figure B8—Standard error of estimates from *x*-bar and *h* calculations for ponderosa pine 1.4E−1/4 EK grade.

Appendix C—Individual Glulam Beam Test Results

Table C1—Results of edgewise bending tests of 8-lamination ponderosa pine glulam beams (Fig. 10)

Beam ID	Width (in.)	Depth (in.)	Max load (lb)	MOR (lb/in^2)	LS MOE (10^6 lb/in^2)	SF MOE (10^6 lb/in^2)
08-01B	3.13	12.00	7,837	5,294	1.392	1.619
08-02B	3.13	11.94	6,738	4,598	1.522	1.709
08-03B	3.13	11.94	5,420	3,698	1.345	1.217
08-04B	3.13	11.94	5,493	3,749	1.252	1.202
08-05B	3.19	11.84	5,176	3,524	1.494	1.544
08-06B	3.13	11.94	8,106	5,531	1.389	1.711
08-07B	3.13	11.94	6,934	4,731	1.338	1.502
08-08B	3.13	11.94	6,445	4,398	1.344	1.553
08-09B	3.13	11.88	5,444	3,753	1.455	1.841
08-10B	3.19	11.88	8,716	5,895	1.323	1.475
08-11B	3.13	11.94	7,813	5,331	1.432	1.630
08-12B	3.19	11.85	7,959	5,410	1.242	1.404
08-13B	3.13	11.94	6,885	4,698	1.392	1.448
08-14B	3.13	11.88	5,615	3,868	1.327	1.335
08-15B	3.13	11.88	5,664	3,904	1.346	1.424
08-16B	3.19	11.94	7,324	4,904	1.781	2.160

Table C2—Results of edgewise bending tests of 13-lamination ponderosa pine glulam beams (Fig. 10)

Beam ID	Width (in.)	Depth (in.)	Max load (lb)	MOR (lb/in^2)	LS MOE (10^6 lb/in^2)	SF MOE (10^6 lb/in^2)
13-01BX	3.13	19.50	13,700	5,627	1.417	1.573
13-02BX	3.13	19.38	9,420	3,920	1.316	1.345
13-03BX	3.13	19.31	12,280	5,145	1.313	1.503
13-04BX	3.13	19.38	5,860	2,437	1.264	1.404
13-05BX	3.13	19.31	12,110	5,074	1.300	1.481
13-06BX	3.13	19.31	9,230	3,867	1.299	1.352
13-07BX	3.13	19.31	9,720	4,071	1.263	1.464
13-08BX	3.13	19.38	10,690	4,448	1.383	1.449
13-09BX [a]	3.13	19.44	8,200	3,390	1.312	NA
13-10BX	3.13	19.31	8,200	3,437	1.314	1.334
13-11BX	3.13	19.38	10,160	4,225	1.229	1.223
13-12BX	3.13	19.31	12,110	5,074	1.335	1.472
13-13BX	3.13	19.31	10,470	4,388	1.329	1.433
13-14BX	3.13	19.50	8,110	3,330	1.202	1.212
13-15BX	3.13	19.35	9,640	4,026	1.417	1.538
13-16BX [a]	3.13	19.30	12,680	5,318	1.518	NA

[a]Long-span (LS) deflections based on manual readings (LVDT data unreliable for test). SF designates shear-free.

Table C3—Results of flatwise bending tests of 13-lamination ponderosa pine glulam beams (Fig. 11).

Beam ID	Width (in.)	Depth (in.)	Max load (lb)	MOR (lb/in^2)	LS MOE (10^6 lb/in^2)
13-01BY	19.44	3.13	11,740	4,866	1.192
13-02BY	19.25	3.13	14,800	6,193	1.262
13-03BY	19.38	3.13	14,310	5,946	1.326
13-04BY	19.31	3.13	13,110	5,469	1.142
13-05BY	19.31	3.13	14,110	5,886	1.362
13-06BY	19.25	3.00	13,110	5,972	1.328
13-07BY	19.38	3.13	10,690	4,445	1.150
13-08BY	19.25	3.13	16,530	6,916	1.422
13-09BY	19.44	3.06	16,210	7,028	1.378
13-10BY	19.5	3.13	11,740	4,851	1.165
13-11BY	19.44	3.06	15,280	6,626	1.327
13-12BY	19.44	3.13	12,820	5,311	1.185
13-13BY	19.44	3.13	14,280	5,918	1.281
13-14BY	19.38	3.06	12,570	5,468	1.311
13-15BY	19.38	3.125	11,450	4,774	1.119
13-16BY	19.38	3.13	16,920	7,032	NA

Table C4—Results of edge-wise shear tests of 13-lamination ponderosa pine glulam beams (Fig. 12)

Beam ID	Width (in.)	Depth (in.)	Max load (lb)	Shear stress (lb/in^2)	MOR at failure (lb/in^2)	LS MOE (10^6 lb/in^2)	Failure type
13-01V	3.06	19.44	18,340	231.2	2,450	1.051	Shear
13-02V	3.06	19.56	11,620	145.6	1,534	0.949	Shear
13-03V	3.06	19.41	22,830	288.2	3,059	1.038	Shear
13-04V	3.13	19.38	20,870	258.1	2,743	1.058	Shear
13-05V	3.06	19.31	29,200	370.6	3,954	1.119	Shear
13-06V	3.13	19.25	28,490	354.6	3,795	0.991	Bending
13-07V	3.13	19.38	36,160	447.1	4,752	0.945	Bending
13-08V	3.13	19.25	27,690	344.6	3,688	1.394	Bending
13-09V	3.06	19.38	32,470	410.7	4,365	1.054	Bending
13-10V	3.09	19.47	23,970	298.9	3,162	1.037	Shear
13-11V	3.06	19.44	33,080	417.1	4,420	1.021	Shear
13-12V	3.13	19.31	21,220	263.3	2,809	0.942	Bending
13-13V	3.06	19.31	37,230	472.6	5,041	1.118	Shear
13-14V	3.06	19.31	41,360	524.9	5,600	0.989	Bending
13-15V	3.06	19.27	30,620	389.4	4,163	1.104	Bending
13-16V	3.13	19.31	35,520	440.8	4,702	1.291	Shear

Table C5—Results of tension tests of 8-lamination ponderosa pine glulam beams (Fig. 13)

Beam ID	Width (in.)	Depth (in.)	Max load (lb)	UTS (lb/in^2)	Axial MOE ($10^6\ lb/in^2$)
08-01B	3.125	11.875	121,400	3,271	1.341
08-02B	3.125	11.875	118,600	3,196	1.347
08-03B	3.125	11.875	113,000	3,045	1.244
08-04B	3.125	11.875	110,900	2,988	1.373
08-05B	3.125	11.875	114,800	3,094	1.446
08-06B	3.125	11.875	142,700	3,845	1.432
08-07B	3.125	11.875	98,400	2,652	1.400
08-08B	3.125	11.875	100,200	2,700	1.041
08-09B	3.125	11.875	100,600	2,711	1.304
08-10B	3.125	11.875	90,100	2,428	1.384
08-11B	3.125	11.875	90,100	2,428	1.222
08-12B	3.125	11.875	106,400	2,867	1.432
08-13B	3.125	11.875	121,900	3,285	1.380
08-14B	3.125	11.875	110,300	2,972	1.488
08-15B	3.125	11.875	151,700	4,088	1.327
08-16B	3.125	11.875	132,800	3,579	1.753

www.ingramcontent.com/pod-product-compliance
Lightning Source LLC
Chambersburg PA
CBHW080629290526
45790CB00007B/2993